COMMON SENSE

COMMON SENSE

THE INVESTOR'S
GUIDE TO EQUALITY,
OPPORTUNITY
AND GROWTH

Joel

Greenblatt

COLUMBIA UNIVERSITY PRESS

NEW YORK

Columbia University Press
Publishers Since 1893
New York   Chichester, West Sussex
cup.columbia.edu

Library of Congress Cataloging-in-Publication Data

Names: Greenblatt, Joel, author.
Title: Common sense: the investor's guide to equality, opportunity
and growth / Joel Greenblatt.
Description: 1 Edition. | New York City : Columbia University Press, 2020. |
Includes index.
Identifiers: LCCN 2020012575 (print) | LCCN 2020012576 (ebook) |
ISBN 9780231198905 (hardback) | ISBN 9780231552868 (ebook)
Subjects: LCSH: Portfolio management—United States. |
Social responsibility of business—United States.
Classification: LCC HG4529.5 .G7365 2020 (print) |
LCC HG4529.5 (ebook) |
DDC 336.20973—dc23
LC record available at https://lccn.loc.gov/2020012575
LC ebook record available at https://lccn.loc.gov/2020012576

Columbia University Press books are printed on permanent
and durable acid-free paper.
Printed in the United States of America

Cover design: Noah Arlow

CONTENTS

CONTENTS

ACKNOWLEDGMENTS

I am grateful to the many friends, colleagues and family who have contributed to this project. Though none are personally responsible for the opinions expressed herein, any one of those listed below could have stopped me if they had tried hard enough.

Special thanks to Andrew Tobias, Myles Thompson at Columbia University Press, Sandra Dijkstra at the Dijkstra Agency, Spencer Papay, lead research assistant at Columbia, and Eva Moskowitz at Success Academy. Special thanks also to Dean Pam Grossman at Penn GSE, Jack Spatola, John Petry, Howard Marks, David Rabinowitz, Scott Friedman, Scott Davidson, Richard Pzena, Jeffrey Schwarz, Jason Garmise, Bruce Newberg, Robert Goldstein, Randall Stutman, Bruce Rubin, Adam Barth, Bernie Seibert, Patrick Ede, Saketh Are, Windi Lowell, Clint Kugler, Lou LaRocca, Yury Kholondyrev, Ezra Merkin, Caroline Cai, Mark Fife,

ACKNOWLEDGMENTS

Stan Bratskier, Tanveer Singh, Jamie Mai, Ben Kolstad, Michelle Tessler, David Erlandson, and Katina Erlandson.

Extra special thanks for their love, support, and wisdom, to my beautiful wife, Julie Greenblatt, Matthew Greenblatt, Brooklyn Greenblatt, Rebecca Greenblatt, Abhi Ramesh, Melissa Greenblatt, Jonathan Greenblatt, Jordan Greenblatt, Richard Greenblatt, Amy Greenblatt, Erica Converso, Dr. Gary Curhan, Dr. Sharon Curhan, Linda Gordon, Michael Gordon, Rex Snow, Angela Snow, Daniel Teebor, Ellen Teebor, Bryan Binder, Dr. Susan Binder, Mickey and Allan Greenblatt, and Dr. George Teebor.

COMMON SENSE

INTRODUCTION

I n the 2005 movie *Fever Pitch*, a school teacher and rabid baseball fan, played by Jimmy Fallon, tries to explain to his new girlfriend why he's spending Easter vacation at spring training with the Boston Red Sox.

> "Oh," the girlfriend (played by Drew Barrymore) says, "you get to train with the Red Sox? Are you allowed to do that?"
>
> "Well, we don't actually . . . we watch the games."
>
> "Aren't those just practice games?" she asks.
>
> "Yeah, yeah, but there's more to it than that. We scout the players. We—we say which players they should keep . . . which they should get rid of."
>
> "And the Red Sox ask your opinion?"
>
> "Well, not yet. But if they ever do, uh . . ."

To be clear, no one's asking *my* opinion. The Red Sox haven't called and neither has anyone else. Yet, this is a book with lots of opinions on which policies our nation should keep (and possibly expand) and which we should get rid of (or at least change)—especially if we want to continue growing the pie while achieving more equality and opportunity for all of our citizens. Typically, a book like this would be written by someone else—maybe a politician or a journalist, or perhaps an economist or academic. But I'm none of the above. My perspective is a bit different.

I'm a professional investment manager and businessman. In a sense, I'm just a guy sitting in the cheap seats. My main skill set involves doing research and then trying to figure out which business models make sense and which ones don't. Though I have a long-term record that indicates I'm pretty good at that task, I'm still wrong an awful lot. Maybe you shouldn't really care what I think.

Still, I can't help having opinions, and yelling at the newspaper hasn't been very productive. Then again, the *Moneyball*-like analytics that now dominate decisions at virtually every major league sports team actually originated from the ideas of fans literally sitting in the stands—not from the experienced sports executives sitting in team offices. Of course, that proves nothing—other than approaching issues from a diversity of perspectives and backgrounds can sometimes be helpful.

Though I've worked in education reform for the last twenty- five years and even helped start one of the largest charter school networks in the country, I'm not a professional educator. But nearly everyone agrees that true equality starts with a good education. So, it should be troubling that our education system is literally designed to be unequal from the start. Yet, as an investor, it's hard to imagine a bigger payoff than successfully teaching children how to fish.

Bill Gates has called education reform more difficult than eradicating polio, malaria, or tuberculosis. While much of what I write is disturbing, I have some thoughts on how we can work around the current system to create real opportunity for students and adults of all backgrounds—right now. Hopefully, you'll find these ideas add a new perspective and are worth considering.

Over the last twenty years, the forces of globalization and technology have wreaked havoc on the value and pay of retail, factory, and most semi- and low-skilled workers across the country. Then again, in 1900, almost 40 percent of Americans worked on farms; now it's less than 2 percent. We've been through disruption before and not only survived, but thrived. We can do it again. But this time, change is arguably coming faster than ever. And not everyone has time for more education.

Fortunately, there's plenty we can do to help during the economy's transition. It just may take a little different mindset. Thinking like a long-term investor, rather than an accountant at the Congressional Budget Office, could come in really handy as we try to help our workforce navigate these new disruptions.

Immigration is a controversial topic. But for the United States, it should be a giant bonus, not a problem. A simple change to our immigration rules can simultaneously help our current workforce, supercharge growth, and confront the challenge of a globalized economy. Though most Democrats and Republicans would support it, our existing immigration policies encourage the exact opposite behavior. The good news is—it doesn't take a complicated investment thesis to understand all the benefits of this change. The math is so simple and the evidence so compelling, an elementary-school education should do the trick. While there are no free lunches in economics nor sure things in investing, this may be an exception.

Pretty much everyone hates banks and Wall Street. (I got nothing here, just thought I'd mention that.) Actually, there are some simple changes to the way we capitalize and regulate banks that should help grow the economy, increase access, and create more jobs. And this time and with these changes, the risks and benefits will fall exactly where they should—with investors, not taxpayers.

Finally, if you think suggesting we "blow up" Social Security is like diving head first onto the third rail of politics—try me. There's a better way for the many to save and gather wealth. Australians do it. We can too. But if we call it "supplementing" Social Security instead, we can get a lot more people onboard. Now, everyone can be a long-term investor.

What the proposals that follow have in common is a simple mission to address two basic questions: If we want to make productive investments in the well-being of our citizenry—particularly those who need it the most—what else can we try? And, how can we use the strengths of our government, the dynamism of our private sector, and the power of incentives to achieve more equality, opportunity, and growth for everyone?

Of course, Thomas Paine offended so many people during his lifetime that only six people showed up for his funeral. Luckily, I have a big family, so even if you don't agree with everything you read, I hope you'll at least appreciate this latest attempt at some *Common Sense.*

CHAPTER 1

GOING TO SCHOOL

I: PAINEFUL QUESTIONS

I was left back in kindergarten. I can't imagine what subject I failed. Midway through second grade, I still couldn't read. Luckily, I was a pretty amiable kid, at least according to my parents, so I had that going for me. Though, for the whole time, I think they were just hoping that I didn't see the need to rush.

It's like the old joke about the six-year-old who had never uttered a word. At dinner one night, out of nowhere, the young boy finally blurts out, "Soup's cold!" His parents, completely taken aback, ask why he's waited so long to speak. The kid answers simply, "Everything's been fine 'til now."

Patience and contentment are admirable qualities for sure—but not if you're really upset about something and your goal is to foment serious change. I'm guessing that's what Thomas Paine was thinking in 1776 when he wrote *Common Sense*, a book that sold 500,000 copies to a population of only 2.5 million (not all of whom could read)—more on a relative basis than any book in American history, not counting the Bible. His little pamphlet professed no patience for the status quo, and its impact was incendiary and immediate. George Washington even credited *Common Sense* with being one of the major influences in winning support for American independence.

So, what was it about this little book that made it so popular and ultimately so powerful? Of course, Paine could have started out railing against taxes and exploitation and in favor of voting and property rights. But he doesn't. Instead, he argues from a different vantage point. Not just taking a step back or even the 40,000-foot view, the power of Paine's pamphlet comes from reexamining first principles as if he were a citizen fresh off the boat from Mars.

He begins (and I may be paraphrasing a bit here):

Where did this King guy come from anyway?

Who picked him? Hundreds of years ago did some ancestor grab power and ordain that all his progeny become kings forevermore? Or maybe back then, the people, by general acclamation or even a vote, chose a king. That's great, but why are we stuck with a decision made hundreds of years ago by a bunch of dead people? Is that fair? Is that moral? Does it even make sense?

The opening of *Common Sense* summarizes more eloquently:

> "a long habit of not thinking a thing wrong, gives it a superficial appearance of being right, and raises at first a formidable outcry in defence of custom."

If alive today, Paine would likely have some tough questions for our country's education establishment. Why are poor and low-income kids systematically sent to the worst schools? If you are poor, black, or Hispanic and entering high school in one of our major cities, why is your chance of graduating college only one in eleven? If most of the good-paying jobs go to college graduates and we care about income inequality or at least equality of opportunity, why aren't we doing everything we can to fix things?

I'm a capitalist, but over the long term, the system only works if everyone has a fair shot. And a fair shot, most would agree, starts with a good education. Yet, our education system is almost designed to be unequal from the start.

In most cities and towns in this country, schools are a local affair. A student goes to the zoned public school in his or her neighborhood. The school is free and financed through local taxes. As things stand now, wealthier and middle-class parents can effectively choose their children's school by paying for a private school or by simply moving to a neighborhood with good public schools. Parents with more limited resources don't have these "choices."

In New York City and other major cities, elementary school kids in lower-income neighborhoods are assigned to their locally zoned district school with other low-income kids. If that school isn't good, most families can't afford to move to a neighborhood with a better school. And even if an individual school were to significantly improve, rents would soon rise in the immediate neighborhood, and poorer families would eventually be forced to move.

One potential fix would be to break the relationship between zip code and the schools children attend. In her 2003 book, *The Two-Income Trap*, Senator Elizabeth Warren suggests a "well designed voucher program" that "loosens the ironclad relationship between location-location-location and school-school-school." Giving parents a voucher, funded by the state, that pays for children to attend the public school of their choice, not just the one assigned to them based on their local neighborhood, would "eliminate the need for parents to pay an inflated price for a home just because it happens to lie within the boundaries of a desirable school district."

Under Senator Warren's proposal, public schools would compete to attract students based on the quality of the school's offerings and by "providing the education parents want." Even parents of modest means would now have school choice. Their children would no longer be automatically trapped in failing and underperforming neighborhood schools.

And, in theory, public school "vouchers" make lots of sense. We should all hope that some version of the senator's plan gets implemented, especially in our most challenged urban districts. It's certainly an improvement over the current system where, as the saying goes, zip code effectively determines destiny.

But this is where good theory runs into a rougher reality on the ground. In the real world, almost every parent whose kids were already zoned for a "good" school would object to losing that preference. In fact, New York City actually has a Public School Choice (PSC) program. But for the most part, kids in good district schools aren't forced to leave, so there aren't very many spots available in their schools. In 2017, 876 lucky kids were able to switch to a better district school through the program. A public school choice program that gives a choice to 876 kids out of the 1 million in New York City district schools isn't very effective. You don't need to pass a math test to figure that out.

So, what else can we do? Well, putting aside the school choice issue for a moment, one thing we should certainly try is to fix underperforming schools. But how should we go about doing that? And even before we set out to "fix" things, maybe we should entertain the possibility that our schools are already doing a pretty good job. Considering the conditions students and parents are facing in our major cities, including poverty, crime, drugs, health, and family issues, maybe our education system is doing the best it can?. Maybe a big part of the answer actually lies in solving some of these other problems first.

The truth is, though, there probably isn't a "first." We need to work on each of these challenges—economic, social, and educational—simultaneously. In fact, it's pretty obvious that they're all intertwined. Nevertheless, granted all the external challenges, if we wanted to improve the education system right now, what would we do? What should we try?

One obvious answer would be to give schools more resources, more money. Of course, the money would have to be spent intelligently. Unfortunately, the most recent evidence of additional government spending to help improve inner-city schools is pretty discouraging. It's not clear that the most recent "state-of-the-art" interventions to fix underperforming public schools work at all.

Started toward the end of the George W. Bush administration and significantly expanded under Barack Obama, the *School Improvement Grants* (SIG) program spent a total of $7 billion in an attempt to improve underperforming schools. These interventions included replacing principals and teachers, instructional reforms, new governance structures, increased learning time, allowing more flexibility, as well as closing or restarting entire schools, among others. In January 2017, the Obama administration released a final report on the SIG program.

In an unusually blunt government version of "we spent a lot of money and didn't help anyone," the report stated:

We found no effect of SIG-funded models on student outcomes. . . . When we examined the impacts of SIG-funded models on math and reading test scores, high school graduation, and college enrollment . . . for all of these student outcomes, we found no significant impacts within student and school subgroups.

The most recent intervention in New York City to "fix" failing schools has been equally unsuccessful. New York already spends the most of any state on education per pupil while offering the highest teacher pay in the country (fourth-grade reading and math scores rank the state 27th and 36th by results). In November 2014, incoming mayor Bill de Blasio announced a plan to spend even more to fix 94 failing schools that had been slated to close under the prior Bloomberg administration (with the students under the Bloomberg plan slated to be enrolled in new or higher-performing schools).

In short, rather than closing the 94 schools, de Blasio's plan was to keep the schools open, reclassify them as *Renewal Schools*, and spend more money—an additional $773 million—to try to improve them. Though the standards used to measure improvement were set quite low, the program largely failed.

By saying low standards were set, I mean low. Under the program, for example, a 1 percentage point improvement on state math and reading tests over a two-year period was judged a success. In other words, a school where 7 percent of students were reading at grade level only had to improve to 8 percent—two years later—to meet the standard for improvement. To be clear, a school with 92 percent of its kids failing to read at grade level could still meet improvement standards under the program.

Union leader Ernest Logan of the Council of School Supervisors and Administrators asserted, "If I told you that we spent $14,000-plus a kid and you know what you only got is a 1 percent improvement, you'd run me out of the country." After three years, only 15 percent of Renewal School students passed the state English exam and only 8 percent were able to pass the state test in math. In 2019, Mayor de Blasio, while still leaving most of the schools open, finally ended the Renewal program, stating simply, "I would not do it again that way." The *New York Times* observed: "The question of how to fix broken schools is a great unknown in education, particularly in big city school districts."

When kids are trapped in a school where 80 or 90 percent are failing, why—it might be reasonable to ask—condemn them to even one more year; especially since each year is such a critical year of development that can never be given back and likely never recovered from? Shouldn't kids and families currently trapped in low-performing schools be given good choices—not theoretically—not someday—but right now?

While every caring and fair-minded person would likely answer a resounding "Yes!" to that last question, there is still a lot of controversy over how to go about providing these "good" choices. One avenue of thought says that we should just keep trying to improve poorly performing district public schools—more money, more resources, more training, etc. Unfortunately, the most recent state-of-the-art interventions in school improvement do not hold out much short-term hope for kids currently trapped in these underperforming schools.

Another avenue would be real public-school choice—Elizabeth Warren–style. No longer would it matter where you live. Students could apply to any school in the state they choose. There would be no preferences based on neighborhood. Ideally, the selections would be made by lottery, giving every student a fair chance to get into a school of their choice.

There are two reasons this option won't solve our problem any time soon: One we already know. Families currently zoned for a good school would object. Many of these parents are relatively better off and better connected and would make for a powerful opposition force.

Second, there just aren't enough good schools to go around. While elementary school students currently have some limited chance to switch out of failing zoned schools in New York City, the best district public schools are, for the most part, filled. Good choices are rare. With two-thirds of black, Hispanic, and low-income students failing the state math and English tests last year, even an average school choice isn't likely a "good" choice.

The bottom line: Most poor and low-income kids are zoned for the worst elementary schools—it's built into the system. We're not very good at fixing them, and it's almost impossible to escape to a good school in another district. Without a good elementary school education, there is almost no chance of getting into a selective middle or high school or of doing well in the middle school or high school you *do* attend. If you don't graduate high school or if you graduate without a good education, it is almost impossible to successfully graduate college. Without a college education, it's difficult to get a good-paying job.

Well, you get the picture. There's clearly a crisis, but as Thomas Paine would say, "a long habit of not thinking a thing wrong . . ."

Over the past fifty years, as per-pupil spending in the United States has doubled in real terms, average reading and math scores on the National Assessment of Educational Progress (NAEP) exam haven't improved at all. So, what should we do? How can we help poor, low-income, and all other kids, for that matter, escape from zoned public schools that aren't doing the job? What else can we try?

II: UNCOMFORTABLE SOLUTIONS

Trying something else was the thinking in 2006, when my business partner, John Petry, and I helped start a new, not-for-profit charter school in New York City. A charter school is merely an independently managed public school, funded by the state and local government. The vast majority are not-for-profit. Tuition is free and admission is determined solely by a lottery open to all. Charters are one way to give another choice to students currently zoned for a failing district school.

In general, the states that maintain the highest standards for deciding who gets to open a charter school and who gets to keep running one achieve the best results. Some charter operators, like Achievement First, Uncommon Schools, KIPP Academy, and Noble Schools, do an excellent job. Others do not. But the decision to attend a charter school is always voluntary. Hopefully, parents enter a charter school lottery when that charter school appears to be a better option for their children.

If the main question confronting our major cities is—How do we create more good schools for poor, low-income, and minority children? then—the real questions for charters should be: What are the best charters doing to achieve their results? Can those schools be replicated and can those methods be shared with other schools, both district and charter?

The premise behind our new charter was simple. If a high-performing school could be opened in a low-income urban neighborhood and then successfully replicated twenty, thirty, or even forty times, it would help show that—with the right supports—poor, low-income, and minority students could achieve at the highest levels. Today, Success Academy Charter Schools manages 45 schools with 18,000 students across New York City.

Fortunately, the schools in the Success Network, run by founder and CEO Eva Moskowitz, are by all external measures performing quite well for students. Most of the schools are located in the poorest areas of New York City, with 87 percent children of color and 75 percent from economically disadvantaged backgrounds. In 2019, over 90 percent of Success students passed the New York state math and English tests, while fewer than 40 percent of similar students in the city's district schools passed the same tests. These results made Success #1 for student achievement in all of New York, outperforming every wealthy suburban school district in the state.

Success students *with* disabilities outperformed district school students *without* disabilities. English Language Learners at Success (formerly known as ESL, or English as a Second Language) outperformed district students whose first language was English on the English exam. Test scores were not affected by race or ethnicity. Black, brown, and white kids performed equally well on both English and math tests, completely eliminating any achievement gap. In short, pretty good results. Someone might even want to figure out what's in the water over there at Success.

Though "trying something else" doesn't suggest we should stop trying to fix the system we already have, charters have met with fierce opposition across much of the country. In his campaign for mayor, New York's Mayor de Blasio told a union audience that Success's Moskowitz "has to stop being tolerated, enabled, supported." At another campaign stop, "There's no way in hell Eva Moskowitz should get free rent, OK?" Within a month of his election, fulfilling a campaign promise to limit the use by charter schools of public-school space, the new mayor cancelled plans for three Success schools to be sited in public-school buildings, revoking the prior Bloomberg administration's approval for use of the space. Why?

Under the Bloomberg administration, empty public-school space was allocated to charter students under a policy of co-location with other public schools. Co-location of more than one public school in the same building is actually the norm in New York City, with most public schools sharing a building with another public school. Since charter students are public-school students (the schools are free, funded by local government but independently managed by non-profits) and charter school students would otherwise be enrolled in traditional public schools, the thinking was that they were just as entitled to use empty public-school classrooms.

In the 2016–2017 school year, there were still 192 public school buildings in New York City with more than 300 empty classroom seats and 72 buildings with over 500 empty seats. So, why was there no room for three schools from the high-performing Success Charter Network? Diane Ravitch, an NYU professor and fierce critic of charter schools, revealed in an article she authored for the *Huffington Post* the "objective" criteria de Blasio used in his decision to deny public-school space to the three Success charter schools.

Unfortunately for Success, none of those criteria had anything to do with whether the school was good at teaching students.

In the 1970s, my freshman-year economics professor, the great Herb Levine, was a world-renowned expert on the workings of the Soviet economy—though "workings" often wasn't the right word. My professor memorably explained:

> I arrived at the Moscow train station at 8:10 A.M. for the scheduled 8:20 train. But no train arrived at 8:20. Neither was there a train at 8:30 or even 8:40. Finally, I walked over to the station office to find out what was going on. That's when the proud station manager let me know, "The glorious 8:20 train came through at 8:05 this morning!"

Of course, the main point of his story was clear. This was ridiculous. It makes no sense for the train to be early if it ends up carrying no passengers. The trains *were* working, but somebody, somewhere had set both the wrong incentives for employees and the wrong standards for measuring success. In the centrally controlled communist system, with no input from customers and no checks from the marketplace, these misguided incentives and standards weren't being corrected. The train was literally leaving the station with no one on it.

In New York City, and in every other major city in the United States, the centrally controlled education train keeps rolling for adults in the system, but most inner-city kids aren't on it. It's almost absurd that school quality—how well the school teaches students—would be completely ignored when determining which public schools (district and charter) should have access to public-school space.

But why is there so much opposition to charter schools, even schools performing well for students? My guess? There are likely a few reasons. First, education money follows the student. That means that if a student gets into a charter school, the government funding for that student goes to the charter school, not to the district school they would have attended. Though charters are also public schools (open to all through lottery rather than by neighborhood), the argument is that charters drain funding from traditional district schools—and most kids attend district schools.

Second, most district school employees in New York are unionized; most charter school principals and teachers are not. Third, in New York City, for example, the mayor has central control over all district public schools (which includes elements of curriculum, work rules, discipline policies, real estate, etc.). He has limited power over independently run public charters. In other words, every new charter student removes money, power, and control from districts, unions, and local government.

Why specifically did de Blasio turn down the three Success schools? According to Ravitch, one of the new criteria for deciding which public schools get to use empty public-school space stated that the mayor "would not open any school with less than 250 students because the school would be too small to meet the needs of the students." In other words, no public-school space for charter schools with fewer than 250 students.

At a minimum, that certainly sounds objective. Unless, of course, I also told you that there is a New York state law that says that if you open a new charter school that has more than 250 kids in it during its first two years of operation, the school is automatically unionized. That's right. More than 250 kids in your school during the first two years? The school is automatically unionized. (How this law benefits kids is tough to discern.)

Since two of the Success schools being denied public space were newly chartered schools, they had to stay under the 250-student cap during their first two years or they would be unionized. The third school slated to be closed by de Blasio, Success Academy Harlem Central Middle School, had 194 mostly minority, low-income, and high-achieving Success students. Luckily, the school had just tested second out of over 600 middle schools on the state's math exam.

From a political standpoint, this high-performing school was probably a poor school to pick on. Making matters worse, the co-located district middle school, P.S. 149, where the Success students were being denied space and where many of the Success students would likely have ended up had their school been closed, had only 5 percent of its students passing the state math test the prior year. With 194 easy-to-point-to kids being harmed, bad press eventually pressured the mayor to back down and he quickly found space for the three Success schools.

But what was the big deal in the first place? Why wouldn't a charter school want to be "automatically" unionized? Well, consider a few interesting data points:

Success opened its first elementary school in Harlem in 2006 with just two grades, kindergarten and first grade. Opening with just two grades was an effort to stay beneath the 250-student limit during the first two years of operation. The school hired a total of 13 lead and assistant teachers to work at the new school. As you can imagine, it's not so easy to staff, create a new curriculum, establish a teacher development program, and do all the other things necessary to open a new school.

Unfortunately, after the first year of operation, the school decided it needed to let 4 of the original 13 teachers go because of disappointing performance. (Note: Eva Moskowitz now believes that with current levels of teacher support and training at Success, support that did not exist in 2006, she might have been able to keep 2 or even 3 of those 4.) Admittedly, letting 4 of 13 teachers go after only one year is likely too many and indicates a combination of poor hiring decisions and suboptimal levels of teacher support. On the other hand, the 4 teachers Success asked to leave in their one elementary school with only two grades in 2006 were more teachers than the entire New York City school system let go that same year from a tenured teacher staff of over 55,000 across more than 1,700 schools.

When combined with a 200-page union contract with limiting work and supervision rules and virtually no effective provision to remove teachers who are not educating students at an acceptable level, most charters prefer to have more flexibility when designing their school model. In fact, the United Federation of Teachers (UFT) tried to show that its work contract was not an impediment to the effective operation of charter schools by opening its own charter school in 2005.

After several conditional extensions, the UFT school was finally closed by the state a decade later as one of the lowest performing in New York. In 2014, just 1.2 percent of seventh graders passed the state reading test and 2 percent of eighth graders passed the state math test. UFT head Michael Mulgrew blamed the state's test-score requirements and stated, ". . . a student or a school is more than a test score, and SUNY's [the State University of New York's] narrow focus on state tests has meant that overall our elementary and middle-school results have not matched SUNY's benchmarks."

At the UFT school's inception in 2005, Randi Weingarten, Mulgrew's predecessor as UFT chief, said, "Our schools will show real, quantifiable student achievement—and with those results, finally dispel the misguided and simplistic notion that the union contract is an impediment to success."

Of course, it shouldn't really matter whether a school is unionized or not. It makes more sense to support great public schools of any kind, district or charter, unionized or non-unionized. After all, there's a desperate need for more high-performing schools in every major city, particularly for low-income and minority children. Yet, charter schools, particularly high-performing charter schools, have met opposition across much of the country.

Massachusetts, for instance, has seventy-eight of the best-performing charter schools in the United States. According to Massachusetts governor Charlie Baker: "Our charter schools are the envy of the nation, delivering amazing results for over 40,000 kids here in the Commonwealth, almost all of whom come from disadvantaged communities and under-performing school districts." In fact, he continued, "most of the highest performing schools in the Commonwealth are charter schools." Over 30,000 kids remain on waiting lists still hoping to get into a Massachusetts charter school.

Stanford University's Center for Research on Education Outcomes (CREDO) stated that "Boston's charter schools are arguably the strongest in the country," with one year of learning in a charter school equivalent to two or more years of learning in a district school (the Stanford study adjusted to make sure it was comparing students of comparable backgrounds). Researchers from MIT compared students who had won the lottery to enter a charter school with students who had lost the lottery. Their conclusion? Charter schools in Massachusetts *cause* large differences in student achievement. The *Quarterly Journal of Economics* estimated that four years of charter high school enrollment in Massachusetts were enough to completely close the black-white achievement gap in both reading and math.

So, why in 2016 did Massachusetts vote overwhelmingly to ban the further growth of charter schools? Charter opponents in Massachusetts (backed by, of all people, Senator Elizabeth Warren and an anti-charter lobby largely financed by the state and national teachers' unions) argued that charters drain local school districts of hundreds of millions in funding each year. How? Simply because school funding in Massachusetts follows the student. If a student enrolls in a charter school, the charter school gets the state funding for that student. The local district school, which no longer teaches the student, does not.

In other words, the argument is that less money for district public schools is bad, period. And that's a fascinating argument. If you believe it, it effectively precludes the state from trying any educational alternative other than the district public schools. It doesn't matter if the district schools are doing a good job or not. It doesn't matter if charters are doing a good job or not. If the district schools teach fewer students, it doesn't matter. According to this argument, money can't leave the district system ever, even if all the students leave.

I'm in favor of democracy, and Massachusetts voters should get whatever they want, especially when it comes to their kids. On the other hand, charter schools open almost exclusively in "disadvantaged communities and underperforming school districts." The only way a charter school gets students in the first place is when parents are unhappy with their local school choice. In effect, parents vote with their feet when they choose a charter school. If there isn't demand, charter schools don't get any students.

Yet, wealthy and middle-class suburban neighborhoods in Massachusetts voted overwhelmingly against charters. But for the most part, charters don't open in suburban neighborhoods with good schools. So, effectively, wealthy and middle-class Massachusetts residents who had the resources to move where they were happy with their district schools voted that parents trapped in disadvantaged communities with underperforming schools shouldn't have the chance to find a better school for their children.

But here was the real tragedy of the vote to ban further growth of Massachusetts charters. When a district school loses a student to a charter school, under state law the district school still receives 100 percent of the funding for the student in the first year *after* he or she leaves. That's right—the district school is paid in full for the student who is no longer there. But that's not all. After that first year, for each of the next five years, the district school continues to receive 25 percent of the per-pupil state funds for the long-departed student. In addition, the district schools are reimbursed for facilities costs and receive additional local funding.

In other words, funding per pupil goes up for district students. In the five years after 2011, the Boston Public School budget for district schools increased 23.4 percent while district school enrollment decreased.

Hopefully, you get the picture. Growth in charter schools doesn't hurt district school funding at all. In fact, during those same five years, district school math and English scores improved significantly both in Boston and the next ten Massachusetts districts with the highest concentration of charter schools.

So, once again, where's the harm in allowing poor and low-income kids to have the choice to attend a better school—a charter school where they have the chance to learn, according to the Massachusetts secretary of education, "at twice the rate of their district-school peers." If the Massachusetts process to compensate district schools for the loss of students to another educational choice outside the district school system doesn't pass muster (and the arguments and multimillion-dollar campaigns against charters don't change regardless of how much extra support district schools receive), then it's hard to imagine any compensation scheme in any state that would be judged acceptable.

But the arguments against high-performing charters don't stop there: Top charters do well on tests because they're just test prep factories. Charters steal the district schools' best kids and most involved parents. Charters conspire to throw out the worst students. And on and on.

Some of the claims are demonstrably false, while others are easy to make adjustments for. Though top-performing charters do attract many of the most informed and involved parents, that advantage can't explain the incredible achievements of low-income and minority students at the most successful charters.

In 2016, 150 new students entered Success Academy after attending third grade at another New York school the prior year. In New York, state testing begins in the third grade. After less than one year at Success, these new students went from 39 percent passing the state math exam at their old school (below the city average) to 92 percent. In English, scores jumped over 40 percent to 85 percent passing, more than double the city rate. Clearly, the great results couldn't be due to Success getting better students or more engaged parents. These were the same students and the same parents. The only difference? These lucky students literally won the lottery and had the opportunity to attend an excellent charter school.

Getting better kids or parents wouldn't explain how Success students with disabilities outperform district students without disabilities; or how English Language Learners (ELL) at Success outperform non-ELL students in district schools in English; how poor, low-income, and homeless children outperform children in the wealthiest suburban school districts; or how students accepted by lottery outperform students who have "tested in" to Gifted and Talented schools.

Throwing out the worst students? Most charters have significantly lower attrition rates than similar district schools. Test prep factory? How about just prep. Many charter students spend 30 percent more time in school than their district counterparts, with only a small percentage of *that* time on test prep. Besides, if a student can't read or do simple math, it's hard to imagine how rich the rest of the school experience can be.

And what about the argument that charters harm district schools? Some studies support the opposite conclusion. How? Apparently, competing for students can actually have positive effects on district schools.

A study of New York City schools performed by Temple University showed that, similar to the effects in Massachusetts, "students in district schools do better when charters open nearby: students in these schools earn higher scores on reading and math tests and are less likely to repeat a grade. The closer the schools the larger the effect." The study also found that the *more* charters there are in a neighborhood, the better the district schools in that neighborhood do on state tests. It concluded that charter school entry produces no significant demographic changes in district schools, including no changes for district schools in the percentage of underrepresented minority groups, special education students, or students that require individualized education programs.

But wait a second. What about fairness? How is it fair to struggling district schools if charter schools attract many of the most informed and involved parents? Let's think this through.

Taking a look at Gifted and Talented schools—are those fair? These are schools that literally test for the highest-performing and most talented students and then, by design, remove them from regular district schools. Maybe we shouldn't allow them to exist?

Or what about good district schools? Are those fair? These are schools that attract wealthy and middle-class parents who can afford to choose neighborhoods with the best schools. Should they be able to move their children from neighborhoods with worse schools? Or maybe they should be able to move, but be forced to leave their children in their old school from the original neighborhood?

How about the best schools in low-income neighborhoods? School performance data for most schools is published online. Should savvier parents with limited means have an advantage just because they can figure out which are the best schools in their price range? Solving this real estate riddle and then actually moving a family on a limited budget takes talent and initiative. How is this fair to the children of less savvy parents if the move is away from a neighborhood with lower-performing schools and less engaged parents? Should this even be allowed?

How is any of this different than allowing parents in low-income neighborhoods a choice to enter a lottery for a high-performing charter school? What if we renamed charter schools "choice schools for low-income parents"? Who would be against that? Or maybe, everyone should have a chance to send their kids to a higher-performing school except low-income parents? If we think that's fair, that's actually great—because that's exactly the way our current system works.

Finally, if you are generically against all charter schools—whether they work well or not—by definition, you are also against trying anything else outside the current system. But what if we renamed charters "trying-something-else schools"? Who would suggest never "trying something else," especially when the current system is failing almost all of those who need it the most?

Of course, it would be nice if successful charter schools were studied, supported, and expanded—not banned, sued, and attacked. Success has been sued eighteen times over the past seven years, almost exclusively by parties with an affiliation to the teachers' union. It maintains a full-time legal staff of eleven and, in addition, has required the pro bono services of at least six outside law firms to help defend itself. Though far from perfect, Success has a record of fifteen wins and one loss. Two suits are still pending, and until Success becomes less of a "threat" (ironically, by its students performing less impressively), there will likely be many more to follow.

Many top charters make their curriculum and teaching methods available online. Success runs an Education Institute to share its methods, and like many other successful charters, each year the charter network conducts hundreds of school tours for educators from around the world. Yet, in twelve years of operation, only a small handful of New York City district school teachers have come to tour a Success school.

In *Mr. Smith Goes to Washington*, James Stewart in his famous speech on the Senate floor contends that lost causes are the only causes worth fighting for. Particularly at my age, I'm not sure that makes much sense. But charters *aren't* a lost cause. Further growth *is* severely threatened, though—particularly in states like New York, California, and Massachusetts where charter students are achieving at the highest levels.

Yet charters, at only 7 percent of all public schools, aren't the major issue. Given their small overall footprint, the continuing political opposition to even the best charters and the natural aversion to changing the status quo, more charter schools won't solve the inequalities in our public-school system any time soon.

So, for most poor and minority children currently stuck in a system that is set up to fail almost all of them, what hope does that leave?

III: HOPE AND THE ROUNDABOUT

At the height of his career, I posed this question to my class of MBA students: What strategy would you use to beat Tiger Woods?

At the time, the challenge seemed insurmountable. Woods had won fourteen major championships. Even other professionals had a tough time trying to beat him. How could an average hacker ever hope to win?

The proposed solution for beating Tiger was simple: *Don't play him in golf!*

When it comes to finding a solution for the vast majority of poor and minority children with almost no chance of making it to college graduation under our current system, the challenge appears daunting. Given the more than $1 trillion spent each year on prekindergarten through university education in this country, making major improvements to the system is, at best, an epic long-term challenge. *Expecting* major improvements over the short term seems unreasonable.

So, if you are one of the ten out of eleven poor or minority students entering a major city high school this year with little likelihood of graduating college, what hope does that leave?

Maybe more than you think.

I was sitting at a board meeting for the Success Charter Network and up on the screen came a chart listing the top 25 elementary schools in New York based on the previous year's fourth-grade state test scores. With over 2,400 elementary schools in the state, making this list indicated that your school had performed among the top 1 percent. The education leaders at Success were justifiably proud that 18 of the top 25 schools were part of the Success Academy network.

The leaders also mentioned that 6 of the remaining 7 were Gifted and Talented schools. Their point was that Gifted and Talented schools are selective; students must pass a test to attend them. This gave these schools an edge over public charter schools, like Success, that accept all of their students through an open lottery. Interesting, to me at least, was that this still left one ordinary district school on the top 25 list. Who were those guys?

As it turned out, "those guys" weren't located in a wealthy suburban school district like Scarsdale or Great Neck. P.S. 172 was a New York City district school in a lower-income neighborhood in Brooklyn with 87 percent of its students qualifying for free or reduced lunch. Jack (Giacomo) Spatola had been the school's principal for the past thirty-four years. I visited P.S. 172 on several occasions and was hoping that Jack would just let me in on the secret. His school's results weren't merely good—they were spectacular.

In 2017, 99 percent of the school's students with disabilities passed the state math test and 94 percent passed the state English exam. Across the city, students *without disabilities* performed less than half as well. More important, that meant that almost every child with disabilities throughout the entire school was able to read and do math at grade level. For English Language Learners at P.S. 172, over 90 percent passed the state English exam, compared to 9 percent of ELL students across the city. Jack's ELL kids were passing the English exam at a rate 10 times better than similar kids at other schools. What was going on?

It was easy for me to understand some of the systematic advantages top charter school networks have that help them achieve such good results: advantages like 30 percent more time in school than in district schools; the flexibility to create, adapt, and improve curriculum and training methods quickly; the right to choose and keep only the teachers they want; and an ability to create data systems and instructional designs that help identify and share best practices across schools with no bureaucratic impediments. Jack's school didn't have any of these advantages.

Yet, Jack's students were achieving comparable and, in some cases, even better results. After decades of leading one of the top schools in the state, no doubt plenty of smart and involved parents figured out how to move into Jack's neighborhood. But practically every single child in his school—with disabilities or without, English Language Learners or not—was achieving at high levels. His school was receiving even less funding than the average city public school. What was Jack doing?

Then again, with over 2,400 elementary schools in the state, only one can have the "best" principal. Given his extensive experience and clear talents as an educator, maybe that was Jack. Most likely, the average school will have only an average principal. So, in the greater scheme of things, how much can the accomplishments of one great school or one great principal mean for a state that has to teach well over two million children each year or a country that must educate tens of millions?

Sure, Jack shared many great principles, but most seemed like common sense:

Every decision must be focused on children.

Every child has the right to a quality education.

Like the Romans, look at what works and try to improve on it.

Lead by example and create opportunities for students and teachers to achieve their goal.

No matter how tough the challenge, don't let educators forget the underlying nobility of their mission.

Jack was clearly an inspirational leader; most of his teaching staff had been with him for fifteen years or more. But he also had plenty of criticism for the current system, much of which we've heard before:

The system is set up for adults—that's the biggest obstacle to all children receiving a quality education.

The system doesn't move in inches, it moves in millimeters.

Each new school chancellor gets rid of whatever the predecessor did—whether some of it was working or not—they stay blind to successes.

Orders come down from the top to "go fishing" over there for some educational goal without any clear connection to the real purpose of fishing—which is to bring back fish!

When Mayor de Blasio's new administration came into office, 2½ hours of weekly instructional time was cut from the classroom in favor of more time for teacher development and parent involvement. My teachers and I thought that was a terrible idea and refused to take away any significant instructional time from the kids. The Department of Education and the Central UFT [teachers' union] would not accept our plan. We resisted, implemented our plan and threatened to go to the press and picket in front of the school. I even told them "What are you going to do, arrest me?" They eventually approved our plan with one slight modification—5 fewer minutes a week of professional development time for our paraprofessionals. So, we agreed. Part of my job is to protect the kids within this building from the politics and other forces coming from outside.

Given his incredible successes with special education kids and ELLs, Jack's thoughts on how we should handle things in this area also had to be valuable:

We base our system on pulling kids out of the classroom to receive special education or English language help. That's crazy. They miss valuable time in the classroom where they fall behind on what is being taught, their lessons become disjointed, and they also miss the chance to master learning in a classroom setting. At our school, we "push in" our extra help to the classroom, we don't pull kids out of class. I got turned in to the Department of Education for violating the rules and not providing mandated services, but we didn't want to pull kids out for 7 of the 25 classroom periods. Given our success, I threatened to go to the media and they backed down. Now, they don't require "push in" services but at least they "allow" them.

And finally, though Jack obviously has strong opinions in many areas, he shared his one fundamental principle for creating a successful school and perhaps the key to his students' achievements:

High expectations for every child.

Unfortunately, that's not how the system is set up. The system thinks in terms of gifted programs, not high expectations for everyone. If one plan doesn't work for a child, we have to be ready with the next and the next and the next. We keep trying until we find a solution that is right for that child. Every school is diverse—each has a diversity of learners. The bottom line is that all the stakeholders must believe that every child, regardless of background, "can."

Think about that. If Jack is right that every child "can," that's incredibly powerful. It's certainly true that almost every child who has the opportunity to attend Jack's school "can," with disabilities or without. It's also true that students who attend other top district and charter schools "can" as well. It's probably not a coincidence that most successful schools share Jack's "high expectations" mantra.

Sadly, most urban schoolchildren in this country don't have the opportunity to attend a great school. Given the overall scale and difficulty of the teaching challenge, a centrally controlled Soviet-style school system that imposes limited consequences for poor performance and few incentives for good performance, and a political reality that makes it almost impossible to close failing schools, this situation is unlikely to change soon. And whether you agree with me about the causes or prognosis, it is inarguable that our current urban education system is unfairly biased against poor and minority children and failing almost all of them.

But luckily, that's not my point.

My point is that if it's really true that almost every child "can," we have a lot to work with! If it's really true that, given the right support, almost all kids are smart enough and capable enough to achieve at high levels, maybe we can take advantage of that fact. Maybe we can design an alternative, a way to work around the current system.

Mark Spitznagel in his *The Dao of Capital* describes how *conifers* (cone-bearing trees) have learned to survive in the evolutionary battle with seed-bearing *angiosperms* (stay with me, it gets better . . .). In general, angiosperms grow faster and reproduce more efficiently than conifers. As a result, they end up winning the battle for sunlight and the best soil. Although angiosperms are able to crowd out conifers for the prime real estate, over time, conifers developed the ability to grow and survive in rocky, exposed areas with inferior soil. At least in this tougher environment, conifers are able to grow without competition for sunlight. Though conifers prefer and grow better in rich soil, overall their best chance for survival is to learn how to grow and thrive in a less hospitable environment. Spitznagel names the conifers' strategy the *roundabout*.

Wouldn't it be great if there were a *roundabout* strategy for education? Sure, almost every child would be better off if they had an opportunity to attend a great school starting at an early age. There's no argument about that. But that's not in the cards any time soon. And as things currently stand, the unfairness only gets worse and the opportunities more lopsided as kids move through the system.

A bad elementary school education usually sets students up for a poor middle and high school education. Poorly educated elementary students don't have an opportunity to attend selective middle and high schools. Teachers in less-selective middle and high schools are left with the almost impossible job of trying to teach students who are often grades behind in reading and math skills. The problem compounds through high school as unqualified students receive "social promotion" to the next grade based on age rather than academic performance.

Arne Duncan, Obama's secretary of education and former head of the Chicago Public Schools, opens his education memoir this way:

> Education runs on lies. That's probably not what you'd expect from a former secretary of education, but it's the truth.

Duncan recounts his experience tutoring Calvin Williams, a rising high school senior and major college basketball prodigy. He was supposed to prepare Calvin for the ACT college entrance exam, and though Calvin was a B honor roll student from a supportive family, Calvin wasn't going to be playing basketball in college. Calvin had been lied to; he was entering his senior year of high school reading and writing at a second- or third-grade level.

Calvin's story isn't unique. In New York City, an above-average urban district, roughly 80 percent of high school graduates entering City University of New York community colleges can't pass the college readiness exam. These kids must take remedial classes before they are able to enroll in courses for college credit. With hurdles like that, no wonder so few ultimately make it through college. And those are the statistics for high school graduates. Over 30 percent of poor and minority students have already dropped out of high school before qualifying to take that college readiness exam. Without even a high school diploma (regardless of its dubious validity), their prospects in the job market are even worse.

Maybe we need some other options. Ready for the *roundabout*?

CHAPTER 2

GETTING AN EDUCATION

I: GOING ANOTHER WAY

In one of my favorite movies, *Planes, Trains and Automobiles*, John Candy barrels down the wrong side of the highway as another driver yells out the window, "You're going the wrong way!" Candy turns to Steve Martin and says dismissively, "Oh, he's drunk. How would he know where we're going?"

But maybe somebody should be yelling at us. The goal of our current system is to complete some form of two- or four-year college—roughly 40 percent of American students now do so. Yet, only about half of those graduates end up in careers that require a college diploma. Translated to minority, poor, and low-income high school students in our major cities, that means that less than 5 percent will end up with a job that requires a college degree. If graduating college with a valuable degree is truly the goal, there's just no way to put lipstick on a system with a 95 percent failure rate.

So, maybe it's time for education's "Kodak moment." Over the last thirty years, the way we've always done things has been disrupted in fields far wider and more impactful than the way we develop a picture. One by one, long-established and entrenched industries and technologies have been disrupted in a permanent way—television, telephones, lodging, automobiles, networked computers, and even books, to name a few. Maybe soon we'll be able to add education to the list.

From the beginning and at each level, one obstacle after another is thrown in the way of poor and minority kids. First, children from families with limited resources are systematically excluded from good elementary schools. These same students enter middle school and high school unprepared and leave high school, even if they graduate, unprepared for college-level work. Between tuition costs, living expenses, and foregone income, college is expensive, particularly so for students from families with limited means.

Almost 40 million Americans have started college and never finished, many because they weren't college ready when they graduated high school. Of the $1.5 trillion of student debt racked up in this country, much of the money spent hasn't ended up in successfully completed degrees. Yet, under law, most of this crushing level of student debt isn't dismissible—even in bankruptcy—delaying or closing off the opportunity for building a family, buying a home, or starting a new business.

Of course, there doesn't have to be a better way. But there has to be a fairer way to allocate some of those good-paying jobs to minorities, the poor, and low-income families denied equal opportunity under the current system. If the goal of employers is to find employees who possess grit and character, good analytical and reasoning skills, and knowledge or mastery of relevant subject matter, maybe we can develop a *roundabout* way to accomplish that goal, even if we end up in rocky soil outside the comfortable lines of the current system.

If it's true that, given the right supports, most kids "can," then we should have a lot to work with. If it's true that, regardless of background, most of us "can," then considering alternative methods for job seekers to demonstrate accomplishment and job readiness should be on the table. And not just on the table, but arguably front and center. If there really is a viable *roundabout*, it would be unconscionable not to consider it—especially for students unfairly disadvantaged by the status quo.

So, what would we need to disrupt the education system?

The late Harvard Business School professor, Clay Christensen, wrote extensively about disruption in the business world. In *The Innovator's Dilemma*, he describes the journey of Digital Equipment in the minicomputer market. At first, Digital Equipment is a disrupter, manufacturing $200,000 minicomputers to help replace some of the tasks of IBM's multimillion-dollar mainframe computers. These minicomputers, together with a team of engineers to run them, are able to handle many important tasks for small and medium-sized businesses.

When the Apple II personal computer comes out, it's viewed as a toy. It can do some simple computing tasks but can't begin to service the needs of Digital's small and medium-sized business customers. Then again, it costs roughly 1 percent of the price of the minicomputer and doesn't require a bunch of engineers to run. Digital Equipment ignores the Apple II and continues along the path that most businesses follow. That is, it continues to improve its high-end product to meet the needs of its current group of sophisticated customers.

Meanwhile, over time, the Apple II and other personal computers are also improving. Eventually, the Apple II, traveling on a different, lower-end customer track, improves so much that it begins to compete with the functionality of Digital's minicomputer. Digital is disrupted by the much cheaper and more accessible personal computer.

By staying on the track to improve its high-end product for its current group of customers, Digital missed the competitive threat from a lower-end product traveling on a different track. Apple and other personal computer manufacturers, by initially serving customers that were not candidates to purchase an expensive, hard-to-use minicomputer and then improving quality over time, were eventually able to completely disrupt the high end of the market.

So, where am I going here? What I'm suggesting is another way for job candidates to show accomplishment and ability that doesn't require a traditional diploma: a new system of *alternative certification*. This alternative certification would be a credential that employers could consider instead of, or in addition to, a degree issued by a traditional education institution. Under a system of alternative certification, companies would consider job applicants who have passed courses or done well on a series of tests (even some in game form) that indicate accomplishment and/or ability that could include analytical skills, subject-matter mastery, creativity, problem-solving capability, or any other traits or skills that employers might find valuable.

The number, diversity, and difficulty of the tests would vary depending upon the level of the job being sought. Individual companies would determine which tests or courses were relevant for specific jobs at their firm. Many of the tests that would be helpful to most employers already exist in some form. Others could be newly designed by outside developers. Companies would improve their methods and criteria for selecting new employees over time.

But the key first step: *Leading companies like Google, Microsoft, JPMorgan, or Amazon would specify a list of criteria (including tests and certificates of accomplishment or program completion) that they would consider when filling specific high-paying jobs, whether candidates held a traditional diploma or not.*

To be clear, these companies wouldn't design new tests or administer them. But top companies would make publicly available a list of which tests, programs, or certificates would be considered when making employment decisions for specific jobs. Whether it was important for candidates to do well on certain tests or in specific courses or merely to demonstrate proficiency in others would be determined by each employer.

Critical to making this all work would be for top-tier companies to invest the resources necessary to develop effective standards apart from a traditional diploma that correlated well with good future job performance.

Think of passing these tests, programs, or courses, or alternative certification, as a low-cost, simpler degree—one that could be continuously improved. Under the current system, to be considered for a good-paying job, most employers require a degree from a good college. Today, even if you wanted to take a chance with a candidate, that would still mean someone with a college degree, but maybe from a lesser school. As things stand now, without a degree, the pitch would have to be, "This candidate has no degree, but I think he or she has real potential!" A hiring strategy like that sounds like an easy way to get yourself fired. More realistically, at many top companies, the candidate without a degree wouldn't even get in the door to be considered for most high-paying jobs.

But maybe it shouldn't be that way. According to a study of thousands of undergraduates in their 2011 book, *Academically Adrift*, Professors Richard Arum and Josipa Roksa found that students in the United States barely improve their critical thinking, complex reasoning, and writing skills while in college. In fact, during the two-year period under study, almost half the students showed no measurable improvement at all.

Yet, in the job market, employees with a bachelor's degree earn 73 percent more than those with just a high school diploma. A high school degree isn't a waste either. High school graduates earn 30 percent more than high school dropouts.

Why do employers value degrees so highly?

Economist Bryan Caplan in *The Case Against Education: Why the Education System Is a Waste of Time and Money* argues that employers value a high school or college degree mostly as a signaling device. Getting a degree signals "intelligence, conscientiousness and conformity," and the better you do in school, "the greater an employer's confidence you have the whole package." Caplan doesn't argue that the value of a degree is "all" signaling or that there is no improvement in analytical skill or acquisition of relevant knowledge going on in high school or college. But signaling is most of it. Caplan figures the split is somewhere around 80 percent signaling and only 20 percent the acquisition of *human capital* (skills, knowledge, experience, etc.).

Your estimates may vary, but the evidence for a large signaling component is overwhelming. Dropping out of school, even one credit shy of completion, costs you a ton in the job market, but very little in the learning department. Employers value finishing senior year far more highly than completing freshman, sophomore, and junior year combined. It's not that what you learn senior year is 6.7 times more valuable than what you learn any other year of college, but you are rewarded by employers as if it is. Why?

Because employers see something else when you complete your degree. Finishing a degree means that you got in lines, jumped through hoops, and ran through obstacles—whatever was necessary to get the job done. In short, you demonstrated the type of conformity, persistence, and conscientiousness that almost every employer would value.

On the other hand, maybe there are other and possibly more efficient ways to find employees who share those same qualities of grit and character. Maybe there are better and more direct ways to improve and test critical thinking, complex reasoning, and writing skills. For sure, there have to be fairer ways to educate and choose future employees.

So, how would alternative certification work? What would make employers consider job applicants who have merely passed a series of tests or courses, but have no college (or, in some cases, no high school) degree? This is an especially good question for leading employers that likely have their pick of top college graduates from the best schools.

Remember, our proposition is that, with the right supports, most students "could have" achieved at a high level in the traditional system. For alternative certification to work, we would have to believe that many "still can" demonstrate accomplishment, ability, knowledge, and perseverance if given an alternative way to do so.

Of course, for job candidates from disadvantaged backgrounds, alternative testing presents some real challenges.

One significant issue is the failed history of the GED (General Educational Development) exam in providing better outcomes for high school dropouts. Passing this general knowledge achievement test in lieu of graduating high school is meant to indicate to employers that a candidate has acquired knowledge equivalent to someone who receives a high school diploma. In practice, most outcomes for students passing the GED are not equivalent to getting a high school degree.

In *The Myth of Achievement Tests: The GED and the Role of Character in American Life,* editors James J. Heckman and Tim Kautz report that "high school graduates outperform GED recipients in terms of earnings, employment, wages, labor market participation, self-reported health, and college completion. Graduates are less likely to use alcohol, commit crime, or go on welfare." Though GED students, on average, have better outcomes than other dropouts, after adjusting for intelligence going into the test, passing the GED does not provide any incremental benefit compared to outcomes for similar dropouts.

Why? According to the editors, "GED recipients lack character skills compared to high school graduates." Bryan Caplan seconds that idea, suggesting that a GED's chief function is to tell employers, "I have the brains but not the grit to finish high school."

What could make the outcomes different in the case of alternative certification? Perhaps, a start would be a more wide-ranging series of tests. Obviously, a certain level of literacy, numeracy, and writing ability would be important to most employers. Other tests covering subject matter, logic, creativity, or specific skills would be helpful for certain jobs. But most important, passing or doing well on tests would have to be only one part of a holistic hiring process.

It defies logic that over 90 percent of poor, low-income, and minority students who aren't currently making it to a college diploma fail to graduate because of lack of character or grit. As we've discussed, most of these students have attended the worst schools from an early age and many have lived their lives with limited resources, opportunity, and support. So, what would it say about a job candidate from such a background who, despite facing these obstacles and disadvantages, has passed or done well on a broad series of exams or specified courses?

Lack of grit or character? Unlikely. (Though it might say something about college or high school dropouts from more privileged backgrounds.)

The more important question for alternative certification would be: How the heck are candidates from disadvantaged backgrounds and substandard schooling going to master a series of potentially challenging exams or coursework?

The answer is that it would all have to start with the right incentives. At the end of the process of passing or doing well on a series of exams, courses, or programs, there would have to be a reward or prize. The reward or prize would be a true opportunity to be in the running for a good-paying job. Another way to think about it: After achieving a certain level of success on a series of exams or coursework, there would have to be a *customer* for the candidate's services.

How powerful would having that end customer be? If enough top companies actually made a commitment to consider candidates who were alternatively certified, what would likely happen next could be very exciting. Once the "prize" of a good-paying job at a top company was established, the incentives would now be set in place for candidates to become credentialed through passing a series of tests or courses specified by that employer as a gateway to being considered for a specific job. There would now be demand for a whole ecosystem of tutoring companies, education classes, and additional internet resources to help candidates prepare for these challenges.

What about candidates from disadvantaged backgrounds? How could they compete?

For potential candidates at different levels of skill or knowledge, each test or course would likely develop a set of *prerequisites*—preliminary tests or courses that should be passed before trying to take the more advanced step.

Candidates at any level of ability or knowledge could now start on the pathway toward passing a specific alternative certification test or program.

Importantly, philanthropy could finally have a real impact. Under the current kindergarten-through-college system, with spending at over $1 trillion annually, philanthropic dollars can hardly cause a ripple. But any tutoring services, classes, and internet resources that would be developed could be non-profit as well as for-profit operations. Communities could even come together to create tutoring services and study resources as a civic activity to help candidates prepare for exams or programs.

Costs of the alternative certification system would be much lower. Tutoring services and classes (both for-profit and non-profit), as well as individual tutors, would not have to be accredited, thereby opening up supply. Crowd-sourced ratings, similar to those for Uber drivers and Airbnb rentals, could serve as real-time quality control. Due to competition, the costs of many internet-based learning resources would gravitate toward zero, similar to the free internet-based resources that already exist. Many for-profit ventures would be supported by an advertising model. Low-cost and no-cost philanthropic and community efforts could well comprise some of the most effective programs.

Big tuition fees and the opportunity cost of spending years working toward a degree with extraneous course requirements would no longer be required to get a ticket to the game. Why? *Because government involvement wouldn't be necessary.* Individual companies would decide what they were willing to consider as alternate proof of achievement, knowledge, or ability in whatever areas were relevant to good job performance. No government accreditation process for tests, classes, or tutoring services would be needed. Nor would any of this require government funding.

Of course, the leading companies doing the hiring could constantly adapt their standards and iterate the types of tests, programs, and other attributes that worked best to source high-performing employees. Most successful and disruptive companies are particularly adept at mining and analyzing data to make decisions. In short, the whole alternative certification system, our simple, low-cost diploma substitute, would continue to improve over time.

Sound like too much of a long shot? Even if a few leading companies were willing to adopt standards and consider hiring from an alternatively sourced pool of candidates, isn't it unlikely that an entire quality ecosystem of supportive teaching services and materials would spontaneously arise? Perhaps. But consider what the emergence of a new group of consumers can help create in even the rockiest of soils.

In *The Prosperity Paradox*, Clay Christensen described the typical approach to helping poor countries in Africa that suffer from substandard or nonexistent systems of infrastructure, health care, governance, and education. Almost all of these countries are desperate for fresh water. Not much can be accomplished without it. As a result, traditional types of foreign aid might involve contributing money and resources to drill new fresh-water wells.

The only problem is that, inevitably, often in a matter of months, the vast majority of the new wells stop working. The local villagers, with their limited resources and knowledge, have no ability to fix them and the wells are abandoned. The cycle starts all over again.

Christensen contrasts this typical failed approach with the history of Celtel. In the late 1990s, entrepreneur Mo

Ibrahim has the crazy idea to form a new mobile phone company to serve many of these same poor, undeveloped African countries. Of course, there's no infrastructure of almost any kind to support such a venture, not to mention that it's unclear how anyone can afford to buy a phone or pay a monthly cell phone bill. With few people willing to fund him and five employees, he starts anyway.

But eventually, Ibrahim figures out a payment system that works in 25-cent increments. Although this is still expensive for locals, it's a lot cheaper than walking three days to another village to see how your mother is doing. Farmers are now able to check whether prices are attractive in faraway markets before deciding to make the long journey with their crops. The demand from new customers for Celtel's mobile phone service not only supports the building and ongoing maintenance of cell towers, but also kickstarts an entire infrastructure of electricity and rudimentary roads needed to service them. In 2004, revenues reach over $600 million. In 2005, Ibrahim sells Celtel for $3.4 billion.

Is it really such a stretch to believe that new demand from leading companies like Amazon, Google, Microsoft, and JPMorgan for job candidates who are alternatively certified would help spark an ecosystem of services to help candidates fulfill that demand? The $10 million XPrize for the first private team to fly a vehicle into space motivated 26 separate teams to spend a combined $100 million in an effort to win. How powerful would the prize of a high-paying career be? If alternative certification helped to provide a clearly defined challenge and a more direct route, it would be great to find out.

Why would leading companies want to source job candidates from this alternate pool? Besides an opportunity to help right some of the inequalities in our education system, or a common sense way to find diverse talent, or the obvious political and public relations benefits for highly successful companies under constant scrutiny to be proactive on issues of inclusivity, having a more diverse workforce is actually good for business.

College graduates from good schools are largely an insular bunch. Choosing only from college graduates automatically eliminates over 90 percent of poor, low-income, and minority students. Yet, many studies have shown that having employees and work teams with diverse backgrounds can bring an increase in productivity, profitability, and creativity.

McKinsey has studied gender and ethnic/cultural diversity among companies and has found a high correlation between levels of diversity and company value creation and profitability. According to McKinsey, "there is a linear relationship between racial and ethnic diversity and better financial performance." BCG and the Technical University of Munich studied 171 companies across Austria, Germany, and Switzerland and found similar correlations. Higher levels of management diversity resulted in increased revenue from new products and services.

No doubt, there will still be many who believe that a plan for alternative certification is naïve, difficult to implement, a drain on efforts to improve the current system, and likely to mislead and create false hopes among poor, low-income, and minority families. You can probably think of plenty of other objections. So, let's take some of them on.

II: GETTING THERE RIGHT NOW

Couldn't alternative certification entice students not to get a college or even high school degree?

The short answer—Yes. Then again, over the long term, if studying for and passing a series of exams or courses or obtaining specific certificates didn't work or compete well as an alternative to a college degree, alternative certification wouldn't serve as much of an enticement or a threat to encourage many dropouts. If alternative certification worked well for many students, then traditional colleges would have to compete and improve their own value proposition. Plus, once again, almost all poor, low-income, and minority students already drop out before college completion.

Wouldn't this whole process discourage students from receiving the benefits of a broad liberal arts education?

Maybe. On the other hand, if studying the social sciences and humanities helped create more productive and creative employees, smart employers might favor candidates who study and test in these subjects. There are over 2,400 accredited four-year colleges and universities in the United States. If you are worried about students missing out on a well-rounded classical education, only 300 of these schools, by definition, are ranked in the top 300. As for the quality of the classical education offered at the other 2,000+ four-year schools or another 1,600 two-year institutions, while many may have fine and valuable programs, it is likely that many do not.

Wouldn't the best tutors and tutoring services for alternative certification favor the rich who can afford them? Wouldn't the alternative certification process just mirror the unfairness of the traditional education system where having more resources translates into more and better opportunities?

Yes. Though students from disadvantaged backgrounds would have several advantages within the alternative certification system, especially if test or course results served as only one component of a holistic hiring process. First, it is likely employers would be wary of candidates from privileged backgrounds who had the means and intelligence to complete college, but chose not to. Conversely, successful test-takers from disadvantaged backgrounds might well be favored as gritty and conscientious. Second, as discussed, without government involvement or accreditation requirements, costs of the alternative certification system would be much lower. Third, philanthropic and community efforts could have a real impact versus the traditional system.

Can employers really use tests to select employees? Isn't this whole thing illegal?

Kind of. Starting with a Supreme Court ruling in *Griggs v. Duke Power Co.*, employers cannot use employment practices that have a *disparate impact* on one group of people (classified by race, religion, sex, national origin, etc.) versus another. For example, if an employer administers an employment test in which one race or sex does better than another, the disparate results would generally be considered employment discrimination. Under the law, this would be true whether or not the test appears discriminatory on its face or whether there was any intentional discrimination on the part of the employer. The disparate results between groups would be enough to create a case of employment discrimination.

There are two ways out of this bind. Under the law, one is to show a "business necessity" in which the test has a direct relationship to the requirements of the job. Of course, this defense should help justify very technical tests for certain jobs but would be risky and likely a non-starter for the generalized testing envisioned under an alternative certification process meant to be a stand-in for a college degree. The other way around the law would be for employers not to administer the tests themselves and not to make the passing of specific tests a job requirement.

I spoke with Professor Samuel Estreicher, director of the Center for Labor and Employment Law at NYU Law School, who suggested than an employer could merely state that, as part of the hiring process, but not as a requirement for the job, it would consider the performance on certain specified tests or courses as an additional credential. Job applicants would have an option to disclose on their application the performance in any courses or programs or on any testing completed at a third-party testing center. This plan should work for most companies and may even be helpful to employers in defending against certain disparate-impact challenges. (Technically, under the disparate-impact standard, requiring a college degree for most job openings should qualify as employment discrimination—but "a long habit of not thinking a thing wrong. . . .")

For companies that wish to investigate the alternative certification road further, a brief white paper commissioned from Professor Estreicher can be found at acwhitepaper .com.

* * *

Clearly, there will be plenty more questions, obstacles, and problems to overcome before alternative certification becomes widely accepted. On the other hand, an alternative certification system doesn't require a majority vote or popular acceptance. It doesn't require political support, government standards to be established, or any government funding. Objections and contrary opinions can be valid and well taken, yet no one or no group can stop it from being tried.

The only requirement to get the ball rolling would be for several leading companies to establish a set of test or program standards for high-paying jobs that would also be considered instead of, or in addition to, a degree from a traditional education institution.

If companies like Amazon, Google, or Facebook were the first movers in setting standards and made a big push to hire applicants from this alternatively certified pool, my bet is that others would eventually follow. Perhaps these employers could even target at least 20 percent of new hires to be from this alternatively sourced group. Right now, the established brand for potential employees is a college degree from a good school—with the degree essentially serving as a ticket to the game. For our purposes and to get things jump-started, these leading companies and their standards would serve as the established brand in the area of alternative certification.

Some of the shift away from traditional degrees is already happening. Apple, IBM, JPMorgan, and other top companies are making a push to hire candidates that don't have four-year degrees. Several of these leading companies already support vocational programs, as well as partnerships with community colleges and philanthropies to train students to qualify for more good-paying jobs.

IBM has a small but growing apprenticeship program for non-college graduates and, importantly, also provides online training materials in a number of technical areas that can result in "badges" and certificates of accomplishment. These can be used for potential jobs at IBM or elsewhere. Other companies are in the early stages of similar efforts as well. JPMorgan CEO, Jamie Dimon, has it right: "The new world of work is about skills, not necessarily degrees."

But having leading companies across industries establish a list of alternative standards for specific good-paying jobs in a wide variety of categories—and then making them public— would be the next important step.

While vocational and other types of skill training can be a wonderful option for some students, zip code and economic status shouldn't be forcing low-income minority students into having only those choices. In a better world, hard work and ability, combined with real opportunity to pursue a broad spectrum of high-paying and/or fulfilling careers, should be the main factors in that decision process. Alternative certification could help open up these broader opportunities and accelerate the process.

And these broader opportunities could come from testing any type of ability, skill, talent, or content mastery. Pymetrics has already developed widely used tests to evaluate social, cognitive, and behavioral factors. Imbellus, in collaboration with McKinsey, is developing game-based tests that measure potential employees' "decision-making, adaptability, and critical thinking." For content mastery, there is no shortage of existing tests. As job requirements change, additional tests can be developed by established or new entrants into the test-making space and employers can source their tests from anywhere.

I have a small investment in a company that has assessed over 20,000 computer programmers on a scale of 1 to 10 for advanced logical thinking, complex programming skills, and technical aptitude. A 6.5 out of 10 on this exam would put you at the same level as an average MIT graduate (based on the hundreds of MIT graduates that have already taken the test). A score of 7.5 would mean you have scored as well as an average Google software engineer.

Even more interesting and potentially powerful, a 4.4 out of 10 on the exam would be an average score for someone with no prior programming experience except for a three- or four-month-long coding "bootcamp" similar to General Assembly or the Flatiron School. Though average graduates from these short programs score lower than MIT graduates or Google software engineers, they still qualify for jobs starting at $70,0000–$80,000 per year. Perhaps a software engineer graduating from MIT doesn't need help securing a good job. But candidates without an MIT degree who score as well as MIT graduates or even candidates who perform as well as graduates of a four-month bootcamp gain a significant edge and can now provide employers with very valuable alternative credentials.

While testing for software engineering talent and other areas of technical expertise (such as health care support) is perhaps easier than testing for other types of jobs, going forward, various forms of alternative certification could provide very valuable information to employers as well as new opportunities for job candidates who don't have traditional credentials. Employers could eventually use alternative certification to help fill jobs at any level.

With alternative certification, job candidates could start studying at any level and at any age. No longer would students be disadvantaged by having missed their window to learn due to bad schools, immaturity, slower development, or lack of support at home.

Importantly, students disadvantaged by a poor K–12 educa-tion, no matter their starting level of knowledge and ability, could get on the road to eventually passing specific tests or courses. The prize of a good-paying job would now be on the table regardless of the journey to get there.

Whether alternative certification takes hold or not, it's pretty clear that the status quo isn't working for minorities and the lower-income segments of our country. As P.S. 172's Jack Spatola continually reminds his staff, teaching is a noble profession. Most teachers are dedicated and hardworking. Many are smart and accomplished enough to accept better-paying jobs in other fields. But insert them into a broken, centrally controlled Soviet-style system, one with almost no penalties for poor performance, incentives for good perfor-mance, or ability to close schools when they are failing, and the outcome will remain predictable. Patching such a flawed system with more chewing gum, chicken wire, and even money has been a losing battle for over half a century.

Sadly, while good charter schools can be helpful, they are perceived as a frontal assault on the status quo and entrenched interests. New York City alone spends over $30 billion each year on maintaining the current system. A rela-tively small band of charters, even good ones, does not have the economic or political resources to avoid getting crushed in a head-on collision with opposition of that size and power.

That's why we need a *roundabout* so badly. Even most large and successful companies don't end up disrupting themselves. Disruption in the business world usually happens from the outside. To expect our public school and university systems to disrupt themselves in the near term is akin to closing your eyes, covering your ears, and chanting "la, la, la" while hoping for the best.

But maybe we have more power than we think to change the way we've always done things. If our current education system is unfair, unequal, and doesn't make sense for those most in need, maybe Thomas Paine had it right. Maybe all we really need to get a revolution started is for a few more people and a handful of leading companies to take a look at our current system and ask a simple question:

Where did this King guy come from anyway?

CHAPTER 3

TECHNOLOGY, GLOBALIZATION, AND DISRUPTION

WHEN THERE'S NO TIME FOR EDUCATION . . .

I admit it. I spent four years in college as an accounting major. Not only does that sound boring, I still don't know what I did for four years. Revenues minus expenses equals net income. Assets minus liabilities equals net worth. That's probably 80 percent of it—takes less than two minutes with time for a doughnut.

Maybe I chose accounting because, growing up, my father would walk around the house sharing his pithy Brooklyn-born street wisdom. Stuff like, "Figures don't lie, but liars can figure" and "Take two and hit to right" (though still not sure how *not* swinging at the first two pitches and then hitting to right field was supposed to help with my homework). But maybe it was because in seventh grade, I spotted Darrell Huff's *How to Lie with Statistics* in the school library (good shot the librarian was also from Brooklyn), a copy of which I still keep on my desk. Whatever it was, I learned early that it was probably a good idea to figure out how numbers work (especially since 54.36 percent of statistics are just made up).

As it turns out, in the accounting world, one of the places the numbers get (slightly) more interesting is when people spend money on things that last a long time. Say you decide to buy a large machine for your business, and it costs a million dollars. You figure the machine should last about ten years. It doesn't seem fair to charge the whole million dollars to this year's expenses. You're planning on using the machine over the next ten years and you'll still have plenty of life left in the machine after the first year is over. So, what accountants often do is spread that million-dollar one-time expense equally over the ten years that the machine will be used. That way, each of the ten years you plan to use the machine will only get charged $100,000 in expenses. That annual $100,000 charge is called *depreciation* and it's the way accountants try to match the cost of using the machine for one year with the amount of sales (or revenues) the business generates each year.

Recently, though, accounting has gotten even more exciting (if that's possible). The world of annual or monthly subscription services has made figuring things out a little more complicated. Let's say a maker of computer software sells software that helps businesses keep track of their inventory. You run a small business and want to purchase the software. But instead of selling you the software, the software manufacturer charges you $1,000 per year to use it. The manufacturer figures that the average customer will last about 8 years. Why? Because once you choose a software system to store all of your inventory information, it's probably expensive for you to switch to another software provider and retrain all of your employees to use the new system.

So, here's the exciting part. What if the software maker decides to start advertising for new customers? What if the cost of advertising to get a new customer for its software works out to $2,000 per customer? Does it make sense to spend that kind of money on advertising? Let's see. If the average customer lasts 8 years, then total revenues over the lifetime of that customer will be $8,000 ($1,000/year for 8 years). Subtract $2,000 in advertising costs and (assuming there is no incremental cost for the software maker when a new customer uses the software) that leaves $6,000 in profit from each new customer. So, yes. It makes sense to spend $2,000 now to get a customer that will generate $8,000 dollars in revenue over the lifetime of the relationship.

But here's the problem—or at least the complication.

Accountants usually can't be sure that the customer will last the whole 8 years. They really only know two things for sure. First, the software maker just spent $2,000 on advertising to get a customer. Second, the software maker received only $1,000 from that customer this year. For this year, that works out to $1,000 in revenues and $2,000 in expenses, or a loss of $1,000. The software maker kind of knows that it's smart to spend $2,000 today to get back $8,000 over a reasonably short period of time. The accounting statement says otherwise. Accountants view it as spending $2,000 today and only getting back $1,000 this year, for a loss of $1,000.

Which is right? You'll decide later. But keep that question in mind. It's really important. Especially since we're about to spend a trillion dollars (that's $1,000,000,000,000—for those of you in the cheap seats).

Before we get to that, though, I want to make something perfectly clear. I'm in favor of progress. I'm in favor of adopting most advances in technology and for increasing the ability of people and companies from around the world to trade with each other. It's just that, over the last twenty years, the twin forces of technology and globalization have wreaked havoc on the value and pay of most semi- and low-skilled workers across the country. In prior decades, relatively unskilled workers could get good-paying jobs in many industries within or supporting our manufacturing economy. As many of these jobs have been displaced due to competition from automation and lower-priced labor in other countries, opportunities for replacement jobs at similarly good pay have not materialized.

Then again, in 1900, almost 40 percent of Americans worked on farms. Now it's less than 2 percent. We've been through disruption before and survived—that's just the nature of a capitalist economy. But this time things are arguably worse and disruption is happening faster than ever. What's the solution for those displaced by all of the changes?

Of course, the long-term solution is education. With more education and training, workers can move up the food chain to jobs that require skills that the marketplace will reward with higher pay. Yet, when you're in your thirties, forties, and fifties with a family to support, a retirement to save for, and expenses to pay, it may be harder to spend time retraining or going back for more education. If you are in your twenties, while more education sounds nice, most workers who have grown up in poor or low-income families are likely to have received a substandard education (over 90 percent will not have graduated college), and it may be difficult to recover ground to qualify for a good-paying job. Plus, additional education can be expensive, and current work requirements may limit free time to train or study. What to do?

One solution would be to increase the minimum wage. The government can just mandate that the least a business can pay its employees is $15 per hour. That would work out to just over $30,000 a year for a full-time job. As of this writing, the federal minimum hourly wage is only $7.25 (states can pass their own minimum wage requirements, which may be higher), so $15 per hour would definitely be a huge improvement. Over 40 percent of hourly workers earn between $7.25 and $13. Raising the minimum wage to $15 can help ensure that those willing to work receive a living wage. And who would want to stand in the way of our lowest-paid workers making more money?

There's just one problem. What if your skill set doesn't justify the employer paying $15 per hour? What if the level of your skills only justifies pay of $8 or $9? How is the employer supposed to make up the difference between the value of a worker's contribution and the mandated $15 hourly pay? Foreign competitors in lower-wage countries may make your employer's products or services non-competitive. Employers will be even more incentivized to replace higher-priced people with cheaper machines.

Having to pay employees $15 an hour, if it's more than they contribute, may make certain businesses unprofitable. Sure, if $15 is the federal minimum wage, everyone will have to pay it and all domestic businesses will be competing on an equal playing field. It's just that there's a limit to what people will pay for a fast food hamburger. With higher prices, fast food restaurants will just sell less. With higher labor costs, many restaurants, retailers, and manufacturers won't open in the first place. So, until more education and training can increase the value of workers earning less than $15 an hour, we need a plan with some other way to help. Waiting for competition from globalization and technology to simply go away doesn't qualify.

The good news is—we already have a plan. It's called the *earned income tax credit* (EITC). It's designed to reward and encourage work and specifically to supplement the income of workers who earn the least. Think of it as a kind of reverse income tax. If you earn below a certain threshold, the government actually pays you something extra on top of what you earn from your employer.

In particular, it's designed to help workers with families. Lower-paid single parents or families with one child can receive a check from the government at the end of the year for approximately $3,500. With three children, the benefit can increase to over $6,500. For singles without children, the benefit is less generous, with maximum payments under the EITC of only around $500. In total, the federal government spends a lot of money on the earned income tax credit, $68 billion in 2018. After Medicaid and our updated version of food stamps, the EITC program is the third-largest social welfare program in the United States.

And what a great program. The earned income tax credit supplements the earnings of working families with low-wage jobs and helps them make ends meet. The extra money from the EITC encourages work by letting workers earn enough to pay for child care and the extra cost of transportation to and from jobs. It particularly benefits poor children. The extra money from the tax credit lifts the families of almost six million children in the United States above the poverty line. Another big benefit: being part of the workforce lets employees gather skills that often lead to higher-paying jobs later on. In general, both Democrats and Republicans support the program. That's saying a lot nowadays.

But maybe we should do more. Especially since researchers at the University of Chicago estimate that the actual net cost for the earned income tax credit isn't really $68 billion per year, but closer to $9 billion. How? First, the EITC encourages people to work. That's the only way you receive benefit payments under the program. That means more people working, paying Social Security and other employment taxes, buying things, and paying sales taxes—and fewer people receiving food stamps and other forms of welfare payments. As a result, the net cost to the government for the earned income tax credit works out to only 13 cents for every dollar spent under the program!

So, why not take it to the next step? Okay, three steps. What if we just had the government make up the difference for all employees who make under $15 an hour? So, if your skills only justify an employer paying you $7.25 per hour, no worries. If we expand the earned income tax credit, we can just have the government make up the $7.75 difference. In other words, if you can get any job, the minimum you will earn is $15 an hour. That's a pretty big incentive to get people working. Don't have kids? It doesn't matter. Under this proposal, everyone who works will be guaranteed at least $15 an hour.

Why won't all employers just pay workers as little as possible and let the government make up the difference? Well, the earned income tax credit is too smart for that. It phases out as pay increases. For example, an employee whose skills are only worth $7.25 will get an extra $7.75 from the government to get them to $15 an hour. Someone who is worth $8 to an employer won't get the full $7.75 extra, but maybe an extra $7.64 as the EITC payment phases down a little bit. That still works out to $15.64, a nice improvement over $15.

In other words, employers willing to pay $8 an hour instead of only $7.25 will still be effectively paying their workers $15.64 an hour (more than the $15 offered by the employer willing to pay only $7.25) and will likely attract more and better workers—just as it should be.

And as long as we're expanding the EITC so that everyone earns at least $15 an hour, we should probably fix some other aspects of the program. First, about 22 percent of the people currently eligible to receive the earned income tax credit don't claim their payments under the program. Either they don't know about them or they don't know how to claim the credit on their tax return.

Second, roughly 24 percent of the people who file to receive the EITC do so either incorrectly or fraudulently. The forty pages of EITC rules are so complex that the Internal Revenue Service finds itself auditing EITC claimants twice as frequently as taxpayers earning between $200,000 and $500,000. Certainly, we should fix that.

Third, EITC payments are received after the work year is over, not at each paycheck. Poor families have a tough time budgeting and paying bills during the course of the year, so money isn't there to pay for food, transportation, and child care when it might be needed.

What to do? Whatever program we propose, it should involve paying the EITC as part of the regular payroll check. This would put most of the onus on the employer to account for benefits correctly. It should eliminate most of the problem with people not claiming the payments they are entitled to, as well as eliminating most fraudulent claims. Also, paying program benefits as part of a regular payroll check should help workers budget and pay bills as costs arise, similar to the role played by a higher minimum wage.

So, how much will this all cost? What's the price of expanding the earned income tax credit so that all workers earn at least $15 an hour, whether single or with family? It's hardly worth mentioning. If we phase out benefits fairly quickly between $15 and $20 an hour, we can do it for just under $1 trillion a year. Given that total federal spending was around $4 trillion in 2018 (we collected about $3.3 trillion in taxes), what's wrong with throwing on another trillion in spending? That's up a mere fifteenfold from the current EITC bill of $68 billion. It's roughly $400 billion more than we spend on defense and a bit more than we spend on all of Social Security. (Okay, maybe it's a big deal.)

Then again, here's where we have to make some tough decisions about the way we look at numbers. If the real question is—"How much do the EITC benefits received today by our lowest-income workers pay off over the long term?"—we may get a very different answer than the dedicated accountants over at the Congressional Budget Office. No offense to accountants, but when they do their job, they don't concentrate much on long-term payoffs. They only know what we spend today and what we collect over the short term. But what would happen if *we* considered the long-term math?

Similar to the work done at the University of Chicago, the proposed EITC expansion wouldn't really cost the government a trillion dollars. Of course, costs would increase because a minimum $15 hourly wage (incorporating the new proposed EITC benefits) would induce more people to go to work. People who wouldn't join the workforce for $7.25 an hour would now, at $15, be enticed to go out and take a job. All in all, that's a good thing but makes the program more expensive.

But then things move in our favor. We would collect additional federal income taxes from more workers and higher incomes, additional payroll taxes (under the suggested plan, employers would pay increased payroll taxes based on the higher $15+ incomes), and more state sales tax revenue. In addition, we would get back the $68 billion from our current EITC program and reduce the need for most SNAP benefits (formerly known as food stamps). Big picture: The increased costs of the expanded EITC proposal would be down below $600 billion.

But there's more. Researchers Michael McLaughlin and Mark Rank in their paper "Estimating the Cost of Childhood Poverty in the United States" have concluded that the cost of childhood poverty in the United States is over $1 trillion per year. This includes the increased long-term health care costs for children in poverty who don't receive proper treatment when they are young, the reduced adult earnings of children who grow up in poverty due to a poor education, the increased costs of crime committed by children who grow up poor, the increased costs of corrections spending, the social costs of incarceration, the costs of child homelessness, and the costs of child mistreatment (social service costs) that occur due to poverty. In other words, if we do nothing, as a nation we are already incurring over $1 trillion in annual costs due to the long-term negative effects of childhood poverty.

Of course, a greatly expanded EITC will not solve childhood poverty, but it should go a long way, perhaps reducing as much as half of the terrible lifetime costs associated with growing up poor in the United States. This could amount to over $500 billion in annual savings. Add in the benefits of lower Medicaid payments to current adults of at least $200 billion due to increased incomes from an expanded EITC and that $600 billion net cost for the new plan falls below zero.

But it doesn't really matter if you believe me. It doesn't matter that we can pay practically anyone willing to work, almost regardless of skill level, a minimum of $15 an hour—and that we can do it for free. The accountants in the Congressional Budget Office will never buy this kind of math. And largely for good reason. If we let every government program spend money now in exchange for huge claimed benefits down the road, we would be inundated with an endless array of new government programs with ever bigger claims.

So, here's the plan.

Let's expand the current earned income tax credit. Let's triple our current plan and spend $200 billion. Let's carefully target families and individuals who need it the most. The minimum wage, now at $7.25, would still grow more than 40 percent to over $10 under such a plan. But it wouldn't really cost the government an additional $200 billion. Taking into account increased government revenues from more people working due to more attractive pay levels; additional federal, payroll, and state sales tax collections from higher incomes and spending; and the lower cost of current social programs due to higher employment and higher pay under the new EITC plan, the cost would work out to less than 25 cents on the dollar—or under $50 billion. Including the benefits of reducing childhood poverty, the long-term cost of this more targeted plan would certainly fall below zero. This is something we should do right now.

While other government programs can claim long-term benefits that may or may not come to pass, an expanded and well-directed earned income tax credit will inarguably put money directly in the hands of our lowest-paid families and workers. It will, in a very direct way, reduce poverty among children and adults while encouraging work and the acquisition of valuable job skills.

If we want to get this done, maybe all we really need is a better name. Instead of calling it the *earned income tax credit*, maybe we should just call it what it is:

Doing the right thing.

CHAPTER 4

IMMIGRATION

Creating Growth and Opportunity
(with help from some new friends)

When I was in elementary school, life was a bit like the Wild West. Cars had no seat belts, yet dashboards were mostly hard and sharp. Kids had no bicycle helmets, yet parents let them ride wherever they wanted. And in the event of nuclear war, no worries; we were rigorously trained to hide under our desks (craftsmanship being much better back then). But even if things seemed more dangerous, at least we had insurance.

Every year, my teacher would hand out a school insurance policy that we were supposed to bring home to our parents. It covered any accident that happened while in school or on the way. And it didn't seem that expensive. It covered a whole series of misfortunes that for the most part sounded pretty gruesome, but boy did they pay. The big jackpot was $10,000. All you had to do to "win" that one was to lose one eye and one foot in the same accident (luckily, losing one eye and one hand also qualified for the prize).

Even in third grade I was pretty savvy. Though I was still young, somehow I knew there had to be an easier way to make money. Plus, realistically, even with my limited math skills, it was obvious you could only win the jackpot twice. (By the way, things haven't changed *that* much since I was a kid. They still sell this policy—honest, I checked!)

So, what's an easier way to make money? What if someone you don't know just agrees to pay you a lot of money upfront and then to pay you a much bigger amount later? What if this person were willing to throw in a bonus? What if, after pelting you with money, they agreed to create lots of new, good-paying jobs for your friends? The catch? There is none. All *you* have to say is "Yes!" Not even "Thank you."

Know any fools who would turn down a deal like that? I do. And they all live in a little place I like to call—the United States of America.

For all its faults, the United States has advantages that most every other country can only envy. Its main language is English, the universal language of math and science and the first or second language for most highly educated people around the world. The country is a melting pot of different races, ethnicities, religions, and cultures. No matter who you are or where you came from, somewhere in the United States is a group of peeps just like you. And for the most part, people like living here. You can travel and settle wherever you like within the 50 states and a few territories, shielded by the rule of law and the protection of body and property. The economy is the largest in the world, with a diversity of job choices and educational opportunities unsurpassed anywhere else.

Because of this robustness of opportunity, diversity, and legal protection, many of the most talented people from around the world would choose to live here if only they could. And maybe we should let them. It may sound too good to be true, but according to the National Academy of Sciences, Engineering, and Medicine (NASEM, if you plan to bore people at cocktail parties), on average, every highly educated immigrant (those with more than a bachelor's degree) between the ages of 25 and 64 who settles in the United States contributes the equivalent of $1 million to the rest of us, right now. That's the current value today of all the taxes this new immigrant and their descendants will contribute to run our government net of the cost of government services they will use.

What if the immigrant only has a college degree? That's like getting half a million. Not too shabby either. Plus, no eyes or feet must be simultaneously lost to collect (and just to reiterate, lose them while not in school—say, at home or while shopping—and the payoff is nada).

But there's more. According to researcher Madeline Zavodny, for every 100 skilled foreign-born workers allowed to work in the United States, 183 additional jobs are created for American workers. According to Bill Gates, internal research at "Microsoft has found that for every H-1B hire we make (a temporary work permit for skilled foreign workers), we add on average four additional employees to support them in various capacities."

So, it sure seems that if the United States severely limits the number of skilled foreign-born workers that can get jobs here, we are throwing away huge amounts of money, not to mention economic growth, and job opportunities for our citizens. When companies can't find enough domestic workers with the skills they need to grow and compete on a global scale, they expand elsewhere. And think of what we lose.

According to the National Foundation for American Policy (NFAP), immigrants have been one of the key founders of 51 percent of U.S. startup companies worth $1 billion or more. In fact, immigrants are twice as likely to start a business as native-born citizens. Research at Duke found that roughly 25 percent of U.S. technology and engineering firms have at least one immigrant as a founder. The U.S. Chamber of Commerce believes that foreign-born STEM workers (those in science, technology, engineering, or math fields) account for up to a quarter of U.S. productivity growth over the past twenty years. Of Fortune 500 companies, 216 were founded by immigrants or their children. This includes Google, Intel, Apple, Amazon, Pfizer, Tesla, etc. Well, you get the picture. Skilled immigrants are truly a natural resource, with the potential to yield an almost endless stream of money, growth, and jobs for the rest of us.

So, what's the problem? The problem is that our immigration system doesn't see it that way—almost the opposite. The United States ranked second to last among developed countries in terms of welcoming skilled immigrants and entrepreneurs according to a survey conducted by the Business Roundtable. That's hard to do. Almost losing to Japan, a country that is largely a monoculture, where fluency in Japanese is pretty much required and where immigration is—literally—actively discouraged, should be embarrassing. (But that's me.)

When we issue our coveted *green cards* (visas offering permanent residence in the United States), we are so restrictive that only 7 percent are issued to workers based on employment qualifications; the vast majority are granted based on family relationships. Our other main option to encourage skilled immigration, H-1B visas (allowing the temporary employment of skilled foreign workers), is an extremely limited, inefficient, expensive, ridiculous mess of a system (yep, also me). In the last few years, applications at the beginning of April for H-1B visas have exceeded the allowed annual cap of 85,000 by three times within the first five days of eligibility. But it gets worse.

If a business does find a talented foreign national it would like to hire in, say, July, it must wait until the following April to apply for an H-1B visa and then hopefully get approval three or six months after that. If you are running a business, it's tough to wait a year or more to hire talent. Plus, H-1B visas are good for only three years and then you must apply for an extension, for a maximum of another three years. Then, maybe, you can try to apply for a green card. With all the approvals, extensions, and government audits, the legal costs and application fees, companies can spend $50,000 or more—not counting the wasted man hours, time, and inefficiency—and effectively wait years to know whether they can keep a talented foreigner as a full-time employee.

If the goal of the immigration system is to protect domestic workers from competition from foreign talent, perhaps the system makes sense. Clearly, rather than go through this mess of a system to hire a foreign worker, companies are incentivized to hire any domestic worker that can conceivably do the job. But is that the right way to look at things? Do jobs taken by talented foreign workers reduce the number of jobs available for our domestic workforce? Does the extra supply of workers from abroad reduce pay for the workers that are already here? Is this really a zero-sum game?

In short, the answer is "No" to all of the above. As we've already seen, every skilled foreign worker hired is associated with the hiring of nearly two U.S.-born workers. The opposite of a loss in opportunity for natives. Pay isn't reduced either. Under current law, companies are already required to attest on the public record, available for anyone to check (through a *Labor Condition Application* or *LCA*), that their H-1B workers are paid at the same level and on the same terms as U.S. workers. In fact, the Government Accountability Office has found the median salary for H-1B workers is actually higher than that for U.S. workers in similar jobs.

Economists at the University of Maryland and the Public Policy Institute of California have made similar findings, concluding that the prospects of U.S.-born workers are not harmed at all. Audits of H-1B visas by the U.S. Citizenship and Immigration Services have found company compliance levels with these requirements at close to 99 percent.

So, why do we send away our most accomplished foreign students, giving most no clear way to stay in the United States after graduation? Why do we reject the majority of highly skilled immigrant visas based on largely arbitrary quotas? Many countries around the world suffer from what's known as a "brain drain." The best and brightest—those with the most talent, ability, and drive—want to leave their native countries for a variety of reasons. The reasons usually center around a lack of economic opportunity, political freedom, and/or safety at home, but these are qualities the United States has in abundance. A Gallup survey found 147 million potential immigrants would choose the United States if they could, almost four times more than second choice, Germany.

In other words, the United States should be a "brain magnet," with the ability to "import" talented immigrants as a natural resource. And we need them. As our citizens age and birthrates decline, fewer workers are available to support our current and future retirees. As technology and globalization increase inequality, diminish the value and security of lower-skilled jobs, and challenge our overall competitiveness, skilled immigrants can immediately start contributing to our retirement system and social safety nets and to the expansion of existing businesses and the creation of new ones. All of which would lead to more, better, and more secure jobs for our existing citizens.

Accomplishing all of this without adding new taxes, increasing existing ones or being forced to reduce social spending should be a no-brainer. Figuring out a way to make it easier for more of the best and brightest to come to this country, so that they can stay, work, and contribute, would be very close to finding a gold mine that never runs out. And it should be easy for us to do. Surprisingly (and ironically, given all its flaws), our current immigration system is particularly well suited to accomplish this task. With only slight amendments, we can even outcompete countries with seemingly smarter immigration policies.

Countries like Canada and Australia provide a streamlined path to work visas and permanent residency for skilled workers—just as they should. They use a thoughtfully designed point system giving preference to immigrants who have desirable qualifications based on age, language proficiency, level of education, work experience, and other factors. Recognizing the precious value of highly skilled workers, these countries have no caps on the number of visas they will issue to qualified applicants under the program. Unlike our current system, *their* systems actually make sense.

But in one important way, our admittedly inefficient and severely limited H-1B system has a big advantage. Our system is entirely employer based. That means individual employers decide which specific foreign workers they want for a particular job, and that's who they sponsor. It's always a one-to-one perfect match. In countries like Canada and Australia with point systems designed by the central government, having an advanced degree doesn't necessarily mean your education or experience will be a good fit for a specific job. Likewise, looking good on paper based on government-designed criteria doesn't necessarily make you the most ambitious or the hardest working. While a point system for admitting skilled immigrants is a clear step in the right direction, it remains far from ideal.

So, here's the simple plan. We should keep our employer-based system. If an employer is willing to pay a foreign worker an annual salary of at least, say, $60,000 and then pay an additional tax of 20 percent on top of that salary to the federal government, then the employer can hire the foreign worker. If the worker completes 5 years of employment in the U.S. at that salary or higher within a 6-year period, the employee will receive a green card (no longer requiring the employer to pay the 20 percent premium tax) along with a path to citizenship. Employers would still be required to certify that the salary of the foreign worker (excluding the 20 percent premium tax) is at the same level and on the same terms as U.S. workers (using the publicly available *Labor Condition Application* process we already have). There would be no limit on the number of skilled foreign workers who could be hired under this program. The minimum qualifying salary could be bumped up with inflation or start at a higher minimum amount if so desired.

What would this accomplish? An amazing win-win for everyone. U.S. companies would be freed to hire the most talented employees from around the world. For businesses, the uncertainty, complexity, and time needed to hire skilled foreign workers would be largely eliminated. Accounting for current inefficiencies, overall costs would likely go down and artificial limits on the number of foreign skilled workers that could be hired would be lifted. Employers would be the ultimate judge of which credentials or skills were most needed. Clearly, if a U.S. worker fit the bill, an employer would hire them first and save the 20 percent tax, giving U.S. workers a large advantage. For many highly skilled foreigners, the opportunity to permanently live and work in the United States would be irresistible.

Current U.S. residents would receive the benefit of all the spending, tax revenue, new jobs, and new business creation these skilled immigrants would bring. The 20 percent employer-paid tax could be used for education and job training for current residents and workers. The income, sales, and local taxes paid by new, highly paid immigrants would be a huge boost to the economy and to the ability to support social spending for those already here.

The good news is that most Democrats and Republicans would be in favor of a plan that encourages high-skilled immigration, especially if it didn't jeopardize the job prospects or pay of our current citizens. The only bad news might be that we didn't do this sooner.

Okay, but what about the Statue of Liberty—give me your tired, your poor, your huddled masses yearning to breathe free? What about immigrants with lesser skills and those seeking refuge or a better life?

From a coldly economic standpoint, according to the same NASEM studies, each immigrant without a high school diploma costs us roughly $117,000. Once again, that's supposedly the current net cost in today's dollars of government services that will be received less taxes that will be collected from these immigrants and their descendants. Complicating matters, most taxes paid by immigrants go to the federal government, while most of the costs of schooling, health care, police, and infrastructure fall on state and local governments. And if our goal is to help as many refugees as possible, according to the Center for Immigration Studies, it is twelve times more expensive to resettle a refugee in the United States than to feed, house, and find work for that same refugee in the safest neighboring country.

But what if we let in one or two more skilled immigrants? Arguably, that's just like someone giving us a million dollars right now (plus three or four new jobs for people already here). No strings attached. What if we took that newly found money and accepted eight or ten lesser-skilled immigrants or refugees? That would be a noble use for the money and help make our country the compassionate beacon of opportunity many of us would like. Others could argue that we should use that money to permanently lift eight or ten children that are already here out of childhood poverty. That would also be a noble purpose for the money.

All I'm saying is this: Regardless of how we decide to weigh the various tradeoffs between helping workers and families already here and welcoming new unskilled immigrants seeking a better life, let's at least agree on one thing—we'd be crazy not to take the free million dollars! The more skilled immigrants we bring on board, the more we can afford to help both groups.

So, there it is. Maybe we should seriously consider accepting all the money, jobs, and economic growth that will come with a new policy encouraging skilled immigration. Or maybe we should all hope to go blind and footless. Even a third grader knows the right answer.

CHAPTER 5

WALL STREET

I: HELPING BANKS HELP US

In the 18th and 19th centuries, the British shipped many of their convicts to penal colonies in Australia. On one of the earliest journeys, over 40 percent of the prisoners died at sea or shortly after arriving. This was a horrifying result, calling for solutions so that a similar tragedy would never happen again.

The shipping contract had been awarded to the low bidder based on a fixed price per head for prisoners who boarded the ship in England, a seemingly reasonable arrangement to keep costs down. But with no additional specifications, the outcome was plainly disastrous. Requiring more doctors, monitors, medicine, and food on board was certainly one way to go to reach a potential fix. So was passing a long list of safety regulations.

But another potential approach was to pay ship captains only for prisoners who made it to Australia alive and well—along with penalties for those that did not. Structuring the right incentives from the beginning turned out to be one of the most effective and efficient ways to solve the problem. And thankfully, "incentives matter" continues to be the most powerful principle behind much economic thinking.

This same lesson from history could still be helpful in addressing some of the issues we face today concerning incentives, regulations, and criminals on modern-day Wall Street. Sure, everybody hates Wall Street. And in all likelihood, shipping it to Australia is out of the question. Yet, the vast majority of people on Wall Street are not criminals; most executives and employees are hardworking and honest.

Nevertheless, we've certainly seen some ugly stuff in the last few decades. Some of it due to illegal activity, but much of it due merely to poor judgment and risky business practices (if that's any consolation). Understandably, the almost complete collapse of our financial system in 2008 and the outright frauds perpetrated by some large public companies in the early 2000s have led to significant new laws and regulatory requirements. There's nothing wrong with that.

But that still leaves us with a couple of important questions:

1. What are the costs of these new laws and regulations versus the benefits received?

2. Are there additional or more efficient ways to accomplish the same or better results?

After the financial crisis in 2008, the most significant changes made to address the flaws in our financial system that helped precipitate the crisis were introduced through the Dodd-Frank Wall Street Reform and Consumer Protection Act, passed in 2010. Dodd-Frank accomplished some very important things. It contained provisions to address the amount of capital required in the banking and financial system. It required banks to assess the riskiness of assets held and to maintain certain levels of liquid assets (those that can be sold quickly). And it mandated detailed pre-planning and created new government powers in the event that individual banks and other systematically important financial institutions lost enough capital to risk failure. These laws and regulations have undoubtedly made the financial system significantly safer than it was going into the crisis in 2008.

The idea behind all of these reforms was that while businesses fail all the time, the proper functioning of our entire economy requires that banks and other large financial institutions can be relied upon to meet their obligations to depositors, borrowers, creditors, and the companies and individuals they do business with. That's not true for, say, restaurants. Most new restaurants fail and that's okay. That's the way capitalism works. Profitable businesses are able to continue while businesses that make poor investment decisions, lose money, or don't earn an attractive rate of return eventually close. In almost every case of business failure, the larger economy doesn't skip a beat. Once again, not so for our largest financial institutions.

That's why many believe the government should have a role in protecting the financial system from failure—but also should have the right to set guidelines and enforce regulations in exchange for providing those protections. Federal deposit insurance was introduced in the 1930s because the government recognized the toxic effect that banking panics and bank failures would have on the overall economy. Imagine if you deposited your life savings in a bank and the bank failed and couldn't give it back. With no deposit insurance, depositors would constantly be worried about the financial strength of the banks where they held deposits and might panic at the first hint of bad news.

But banks lend out much of the money they receive in deposits to long-term borrowers like homeowners and corporations. If depositors demanded their money back all at once, most banks couldn't liquidate those long-term loans to meet the demand. Without deposit insurance, depositors who panicked first might get paid back, while others might not. In addition, banks would no longer be able to make as many long-term loans. Banks would have to charge more for the loans they did make, as depositors would want to get paid more for deposits that were uninsured and now much riskier. Borrowing costs for businesses and individuals would likely be much higher.

In short, having the government act as a backstop to help insure deposits and avoid the many potential costs of failure has been a great contributor to keeping our financial system functioning properly and efficiently. It's been good for everybody—banks, borrowers, depositors, and the entire economic system.

But the 2008 crisis and the seriousness of the economic downturn that followed not only reinforced the systemic importance of keeping large players within our financial system solvent and operating, but also laid bare some of the growing but underappreciated risks within the system. One of the risks that became clearer is just how interconnected our banking and financial systems actually are. Banks do business not only with one another on a daily basis but with other large financial institutions such as insurance companies and investment firms.

Over the decades preceding the crisis, the effects of increased globalization, the extensive use of derivatives and other financial innovations, and expanding securitization (where loans to multiple borrowers are packaged together and sold to unrelated financial institutions—helping to spread risks widely) had accelerated this level of interconnection. It became clear after the crisis that financial institutions are so interconnected that the failure of even one large financial institution could affect the proper functioning of the entire economy.

The 2008 crisis also helped underscore, yet again, the underlying nature of the banking business. It's competitive.

Banks are almost wired to get into trouble. To a borrower, one bank's money is as good as another. To an insured depositor, the bank that pays the most interest is often the most attractive. As a result, banks often compete on how much they pay their depositors, how little they charge borrowers, or how easy their lending terms are. To compound the potential problems, lending is often concentrated in the same hot sectors. Cheap loans made on easy terms (with few covenants or little collateral) in many of the same areas can still work out well for a bank when the economy is good, but in an economic downturn, when real estate prices fall and business cash flows dry up, they tend to cause problems.

And taking loan losses from time to time would still be okay, except that banks are incredibly leveraged. Banks don't really have much equity capital underlying all of their assets, so there's not a lot of room for error. At one of the largest and best capitalized banks in the United States, JPMorgan Chase, the ratio of tangible common equity to total assets was just 7% at the end of 2018, ten years after the 2008 crisis. Add in 1% more for preferred equity (we'll discuss this later), and that's still like putting $80,000 down, borrowing $920,000, and buying a house that costs a million dollars. A small drop in the value of the house could easily wipe out all, or a large portion, of that sliver of equity capital. Then again, the ratio of tangible common equity to total assets for JPMorgan was much lower in 2008, just 4%, so we're clearly in better shape than we were before the crisis. But is better good enough?

Many would argue yes. Since the crisis, much more was accomplished through Dodd-Frank, in terms of new regulations, and heightened standards than simply requiring increased equity capital. All of these changes helped address the risk that the failure of a single major financial institution could put the entire financial system at risk.

First, strict new risk assessment standards for each type of asset held by banks were required. In addition to comparing a bank's equity cushion to a bank's total assets, banks were required to bucket assets held based on relative risk. Securities like U.S. Treasury bills were viewed as low-risk assets (with no chance of default), while certain subordinated debt and unsecured loans held by the bank were viewed as increasing risk. For example, at the end of 2018, while JPMorgan's assets totaled over $2.6 trillion, the high quality of many of those assets made the assessment of risk-weighted assets (RWA) only $1.5 trillion. That meant that while the ratio of tangible common equity to total assets was 7%, properly accounting for the lower risk of assets held took the ratio of tangible common equity relative to risk-weighted assets to over 12%. Though putting up $120,000 and borrowing $880,000 is still quite leveraged, many believe this should still be an ample equity cushion against a fall in asset values during the next crisis.

Second, even if a bank's tangible equity did get wiped out in the next economic crisis, under the new regulations, certain long-term debt owed by the bank would immediately become eligible to be converted into new equity. In the

2008 crisis, this immediate conversion of a bank's debt into new equity was not an option. While a debt holder's claims against a failed company are often converted into equity in a normal bankruptcy, this can take months or years. In a financial crisis, there's no time for that. If a large bank or financial institution can't meet its obligations, even for a day, the harm can cascade throughout our highly interconnected financial system almost immediately.

That's why after the failure of Lehman Brothers in 2008, the federal government was forced to provide financial support to many of the largest financial institutions in the country. Without this support, the financial crisis would almost certainly have been far more devastating. But that's not fair. Shareholders and debt holders of large financial institutions shouldn't enjoy all the profits when a company does well and let the federal government (and all the taxpayers) bail them out whenever a crisis hits. But effectively, that's what happened in 2008.

To avoid having such an unfair scenario ever happen again, regulators have been granted some new powers. Now, as a result of Dodd-Frank and the new regulations that followed, when a bank loses enough of its equity capital to be deemed failing, regulators have the power to place the bank in receivership and immediately convert its subordinated and unsecured debt into new equity. This debt that can be immediately converted into equity is known as *bail-inable* debt. This wasn't possible in 2008. But at the end of 2018, JPMorgan had not only $185 billion in tangible common equity and $26 billion in preferred equity, but an additional $171 billion in bail-inable debt.

What that all adds up to is this: Though JPMorgan's ratio of tangible common equity (plus preferred stock) to total assets appears to be only 8%, that's not a fair picture of how much cushion the bank has before the federal government (read: taxpayers) might be forced to step in and bail it out in the next crisis. Add in another $171 billion of bail-inable debt that can immediately be converted to equity, if needed, and that cushion climbs to 14.5% of total assets. But adjust for risk-weighted assets of only $1.5 trillion (perhaps a better measure of assets actually at risk), and JPMorgan would have a cushion of tangible equity plus bail-inable debt (known as *Total Loss Absorbing Capacity* or *TLAC*) of over 25% relative to its risk-weighted assets. That's arguably plenty of protection against the government ever having to step in again. Problem solved. Case closed.

Though some beg to differ. Current Federal Reserve Bank of Minneapolis president Neel Kashkari does. Kashkari worked for the U.S. Treasury Department during the 2008 crisis and helped in negotiations for the takeover of the Bear Stearns investment firm before it collapsed and was then put in charge of the federal government's *Troubled Asset Relief Program* (TARP). TARP was a $700 billion federal program designed to buy up distressed assets and intended to help support the prices of assets owned by banks and other financial institutions. Suffice it to say, Kashkari has experience in understanding how government regulators react in the midst of a real financial crisis. And he has some concerns about how prepared we are for the next one.

In particular, he's worried about banks that are considered too big to fail (TBTF). These are banks that are so big that the prospect of failure would be catastrophic for the financial system and the government would have no choice but to bail them out again should they run into trouble. What are the odds this becomes necessary under current regulations? After a two-year study, the Minneapolis Fed calculated that over the next century, the odds have dropped from 84 percent before the 2008 crisis down to 67 percent as a result of Dodd-Frank and the other new regulations and restrictions that have followed. Not all that comforting.

According to the Minneapolis study, even if we more than doubled current equity capital requirements to 23.5% of risk-weighted assets, the odds of a bailout would only drop to 39 percent. It would take raising equity capital requirements for these large banks to over 38% of risk-weighted assets (and over 23% of total assets) to bring the odds of a required bailout under 10 percent. That's almost four times the equity capital that we currently require—something no big bank would do. And that's Kashkari's point. He wants to break up these large banks by making capital requirements for them so prohibitive that no bank will want to be deemed "too big to fail." In effect, he wants them to voluntarily downsize over time so that they are no longer a threat to the system in the event they fail in the future.

But what about the "bail-inable" debt? In JPMorgan's case, its equity plus bail-inable debt (debt that can be converted into equity, if needed) is already over 25% of risk-weighted assets. But in a time of economic stress during the next big crisis, Kashkari doesn't believe the government would actually make debtholders of these huge banks take any loss by forcing a conversion into equity. In fact, even in the case of several smaller European banks that have failed in recent years, government regulators have chosen not to force losses on holders of bail-inable debt. His Minneapolis study states: "We have no reason to believe that the government will follow through on its current plan in the next crisis because imposing losses on debtholders of TBTF banks in a weak environment will be viewed as too risky and complex with a high likelihood of intensifying a crisis."

Stanford professor of finance and economics and coauthor of *The Bankers' New Clothes* Anat Admati agrees. In a crisis situation where a bank that is considered TBTF gets close to losing most of its equity capital, forcing debtholders of the bank to take a loss could create even more instability. Kashkari and Admati would argue that once bondholders of a major bank were forced to take a loss, contagion across the system could ensue. Creditors of other large banks might fear the same could happen and then try to pull their funding. The panic might be hard to stop.

So, what else can we do?

II: THE PRISONER'S SOLUTION

Maybe stricter regulation along with more inspections and supervision is the best answer. You know—more rules, more monitors, and a longer list of restraints and restrictions. Then again, we've already done a lot of that. But this extra regulation has come at a price with some significant collateral damage. One result has been less access to credit for smaller and new businesses. Not only are small business loans considered riskier, requiring more bank capital under the new rules, but more regulation has made it tougher for the small banks who make many of these loans to compete. While larger banks can better handle the increased regulatory costs, smaller banks can't afford the extra staff and expense.

Though some regulatory relief for smaller banks has been enacted in recent years, it's not enough. In fact, Dodd-Frank and other regulations have made it so difficult for small banks that the number of new bank charters issued each year has fallen by over 90 percent since before the 2008 crisis. And that's not good news for small business. Since 2010, commercial and industrial loans of less than $1 million for small businesses have plunged while at the same time bank loans for larger businesses that borrow over $1 million have almost doubled. More troublingly, net small business formation has dropped off drastically (75 percent or more) since the crisis began. That's devastating to economic growth and likely in part a result of reduced access to credit for small and new businesses.

In sum, more rules and regulations haven't solved all of the problems for large banks and new problems have been created for small ones. If we stay on this course, we may still have to bail out banks considered too big to fail while we continue to strangle smaller banks and businesses—jeopardizing our future growth. In other words, maybe it's time to start thinking about Australian prisoners and British sea captains.

An alternative approach to even more fiddling with our Rube Goldberg–like, finger-in-the-dike patchwork of regulations, supervisory authorities, and emergency contingency plans would be to restructure the incentives within the banking system from the beginning. What that means is doing a better job of setting banks up for long-term success at the start but also aligning things so that the risks of failure and the benefits of success fall exactly where they should. And what that really means is that banks need more equity capital.

But don't stop reading yet. . . .

No doubt, every banking executive and bank investor just got very upset. I understand their pain, but even *they* should read on. Banks play a very important role in keeping our economic system functioning and our economy growing. If we pile on too many regulations and make capital requirements too onerous, at some point, borrowing from a bank would become extraordinarily expensive while investing in the banking business would become much less attractive. In other words, we can make things so tough in order to fix one problem or another, almost no one will want to do the important work of banking.

And the reason most banks will fight being forced to raise more equity capital is simple—they'll earn much lower returns on capital. Think about it this way:

Buy a house for a million dollars. Rent it out for $50,000 a year (net of the expenses to run the house). If you put up $100,000 of your own capital to buy the house and then borrow $900,000 at 4%, your cost of financing is $36,000 per year. Collecting $50,000 in net rent and then subtracting financing costs of $36,000 still leaves you with $14,000 in net profit. Dividing the $14,000 in profit by the $100,000 in capital you invested gives you a return of 14% on your capital ($14,000/$100,000 = 14%). Pretty good.

But what if instead of putting up 10 percent of the cost of the million-dollar house, you now have to put up 20 percent, or $200,000. Now the math works this way:

Buy a house for a million dollars. Rent it out for $50,000 a year. Put up $200,000 of your own capital and borrow $800,000 at 4%. Your financing cost is now $32,000 per year. Collecting $50,000 in net rent and then subtracting financing costs of $32,000 leaves you with $18,000 in profit. Dividing the $18,000 in profit by the $200,000 in capital you invested gives you a return of 9% on your capital ($18,000/$200,000 = 9%).

Putting up only 10 percent on the purchase price of the house, instead of 20 percent, gets you an increased return on capital of 14% versus only 9%, a return on capital more than 50 percent higher.

And now you get it.

Banks would rather put up 10 percent in equity capital relative to their total assets than 20 percent. If we force banks to double or even triple how much equity capital they must pony up to do the same amount of business (as both Kashkari and Admati would suggest), bank returns on equity capital would fall drastically. Yes, the risk of bank failures would almost be eliminated and the need for hyper-protective regulation would be greatly diminished, but at some point, banks would likely have to start charging borrowers more and would still end up earning lower returns on equity capital. Not great news for banks, borrowers, or the economy.

So, here's the plan. Let's require banks to raise more equity capital, perhaps bringing total equity capital to between 20% and 30% of total assets. But, in place of bail-inable debt, let's let them raise that added equity capital through a new kind of preferred stock.

Preferred stock isn't debt. In general, owners of preferred stock are entitled to a set dividend payment that must be paid before common shareholders receive their dividends. In most cases, if a company can't pay a preferred dividend or chooses not to, nothing happens. Preferred stock shareholders can't force a company into bankruptcy if they go unpaid. In the case of *cumulative preferred stock*, unpaid dividends cumulate until the company is able to pay. No new dividends can be paid to common shareholders until preferred shareholders receive all the dividends they are entitled to. But that's it.

The advantages for a company to issue debt instead of preferred stock are usually two-fold. First, interest payments on debt are often totally or at least partially tax deductible against a company's income; preferred dividends are usually not. That may make it cheaper for banks to take on debt rather than issue preferred stock. Second, since debt is senior in priority for payback over preferred stock, taking on debt rather than issuing preferred stock can often end up being a cheaper way to raise money.

But what if we work on that? Let's make it cheaper for a bank to raise money through issuing preferred stock. Let's make the dividends on preferred stock issued by banks fully deductible for tax purposes against a bank's income. Next, let's make owning preferred stock issued by a bank more attractive by making the dividends tax-free to the holder of the preferred. That's it!

Why should we do all this? Well, owners of common and preferred stocks lose money all the time. Stocks go up and stocks go down; that's just part of the system. Owners of common and preferred stocks are willing providers of equity capital and know the risks involved: the value of their holdings could fall or they may not receive as much in dividends as they hoped. They also know that if they don't get what they originally expected, they have no right to force a company to pay dividends or to file for bankruptcy.

If banks start out with 20–30% of their total assets provided by equity capital, making bad loans or bad decisions won't matter very much. Virtually all losses will be the problem of stockholders, either common or preferred. It won't be the government's problem and losses won't fall on taxpayers or depositors. The risks will now fall almost exclusively just where they should—with equity holders. Sort of like what happens when a restaurant fails.

But wait. Isn't this just a direct handout to banks and to the owners of bank equity securities? Well, yes, absolutely! But we already support banks that are considered too big to fail (likely a longer list than we like to acknowledge) by being an implicit backstop in the event of another major financial crisis. We support smaller banks (which usually lend within their communities and to smaller businesses) with federal deposit insurance. We do these things because we believe it benefits all of us and our entire economy to have a reliable, functioning banking system.

But at least now, if we require banks to have much more equity capital right from the start, the odds that taxpayers will ever have to pick up the tab in a crisis (if the Minneapolis Fed estimates are close to correct) should fall by a factor of six or seven times. An enhanced equity cushion should provide our community banks more flexibility to lend to small businesses. With loan losses now falling almost exclusively on equity holders, rules and regulations can be adjusted to reflect a new buffer of equity capital two to three times as large as under current rules. Yes, a new tax-advantaged preferred stock will be a benefit to banks and bank equity holders, but it should set up the risks, rewards, and incentives within our banking system to be more direct, more efficient, and fairer than what we have right now.

To make sure incentives stay where they should, a bank's board of directors should have a fiduciary duty to maximize the combined value of both the common stock and the new preferred stock (as if they were stapled together as one security). Management stock options should also be based on the combined value of both securities. Board representation should be apportioned between both securities as well.

Shareholders can buy just common stock or just preferred stock or a combination of both. Common shareholders will potentially receive their leveraged return on common equity and preferred shareholders their preferred standing to receive set dividends (you pays your money and you takes your chances). But we want management and directors to be incentivized to protect the value of all of a bank's equity in a distressed environment, not just the common shares. This is the best way for depositors and taxpayers to receive the full benefit of the new increased level of equity investment jointly being made by common and preferred shareholders.

One more thing. As far as we know, humans are the only species that will actually sacrifice their lives on behalf of ideas or principles that are important to them. I love this idea for recapitalizing banks with more equity. I think it can make our banking system stronger and simultaneously support increased economic growth for large and small businesses while keeping the risks where they belong. On the other hand (and as much as I would appreciate the support), even if you could find a creative way to sacrifice yourself while somehow advancing the cause of this new tax-advantaged preferred stock for banks, please, stick around and read the next chapter first.

CHAPTER 6

SAVING TIME AND SOCIAL SECURITY

NOW EVERYONE CAN BE A LONG-TERM INVESTOR

So, a few years ago, I was asked to teach a class on investing once a week to a group of ninth graders from Harlem. I eagerly said yes and immediately began to have second thoughts. For over two decades, I'd been teaching a course on investing at an Ivy League business school. After teaching for so long, I knew what I was doing (more or less). Making things even easier, the MBAs knew what they were doing too, with an average age of 27 and three or four years of work experience before getting to me. Teaching a bunch of ninth graders was going to be tougher.

With no money to invest and still years away from a good-paying job, most teenagers don't care about investing. I wanted them to. I'm pretty sure they just wanted to go to lunch. Undaunted, the first day of class I handed out loose-leaf binders with two charts on the front cover.

One chart had a column of numbers labeled "Investor A" at the top. In this first chart, Investor A invests $2,000 each year into a retirement account starting at age 26. This same investor continues to make annual contributions to his retirement account until age 65, achieving a return of 10 percent per year on his investments. That works out to 40 annual contributions of $2,000.

In the next column, "Investor B" begins at an earlier age. Investor B starts investing $2,000 each year at age 19 and also achieves a 10 percent annual return on his investments. But Investor B only contributes $2,000 each year for 7 years and stops contributing at age 26 (just when Investor A is getting started). That's only 7 annual contributions of $2,000.

At age 65, who ends up with more money? Investor A or Investor B? The surprise is that Investor B, the one who made just 7 annual contributions when he was young and then never contributed again after age 26, ends up with more money at 65—$930,641 to be exact. Investor A, who diligently made contributions each year for over 40 years, ends up with less —$893,704. Not bad for Investor A, but not my point.

The point is this: When it comes to saving, investing, and the power of compounding, starting earlier is better—a lot better. But most people don't. And it's pretty obvious why.

Adults have lots of expenses—rent and mortgage payments, children, food, clothing, student debt—and saving for retirement doesn't usually make the list of immediate needs. According to Monique Morrissey, an economist at the Economic Policy Institute (EPI), nearly half of all working-age families have zero retirement savings; the median family between the ages of 32 and 61 has saved only $5,000. The typical working-age, lower-income, black, Hispanic, or non-college-educated family has no retirement account savings at all. Almost 40 percent of Americans, according to one well-publicized study, can't meet a $400 emergency expense without borrowing or selling something.

So, forget about starting early; many aren't starting at all.

But I know what you're thinking. What about Australia? Funny you should ask. Australians have been much better about building up their retirement savings. In a program called *superannuation*, Australians have already collectively saved the equivalent of over 2 trillion U.S. dollars. While that might sound like pocket change to you (assuming you're delusional), there aren't that many people in Australia. If we adjust for the relative size of the U.S., that would be like Americans saving almost $30 trillion for retirement in superannuation accounts—close to the combined value of every publicly traded company in the United States. That's a lot of savings.

How do Australians do it? Are they just more disciplined than Americans? Almost certainly not. They don't have to be. Fortunately for them, Australians are literally forced to save. Or more accurately, their employers are forced to save on their behalf. Employers in Australia must contribute an amount equal to 9.5 percent (growing to 12 percent by 2025) of each employee's wages and salary to a superannuation fund chosen by the employee.

Collectively, Australians have over 500 professionally managed superannuation funds to choose from. Much of the money contributed can then be channeled back into stocks, bonds, infrastructure, real estate, and the private economy. In most cases, citizens can even voluntarily add additional amounts to the contributions made by their employer. In general, superannuation contributions are tax-deductible for the employer and non-taxable for the employee. So far so good.

But what if that's still not enough savings to carry Australians through retirement? After all, superannuation only started in the early 1990s, not enough time for many current retirees to accumulate sufficient savings. Luckily, or perhaps prudently, Australia also has an *Age Pension* that is designed to supplement superannuation savings in the event retirees don't have enough wealth or income to make it through retirement. So, there we have it. Australia's retirement system provides for privately controlled retirement accounts supplemented by the government in case that's not enough. Pretty good for them.

What about us? In the United States, we have Social Security. Social Security is also pretty good. Employers and employees each contribute 6.2 percent of wages and salary (12.4 percent in total) to the government in exchange for promised retirement or disability benefits later on. The size of benefits received is related to the size of contributions made. Workers earning roughly $50,000, if they retire at 62, receive approximately $15,000 back each year in retirement benefits, or around 30 percent of their working wages. Those with lower incomes receive a slightly higher percentage of working wages, or about 40 percent. That works out to about $9,000 each year for someone with wages of $22,000.

Though the income from Social Security payments is incredibly important for most retirees—many can't live without them—the size of payments isn't particularly generous at lower income levels. But even at this limited level of benefits, our Social Security system isn't very well funded. It's essentially a pay-as-you-go system where Social Security contributions from current workers are paid out to current retirees.

Yes, we do have a Social Security "trust fund" (invested in U.S. government bonds) that mostly serves to level out fluctuations of contributions due to baby booms and busts, but at the current pace of contributions and payouts, that fund will be gone in about 15 years. As our population ages and the ratio of Social Security recipients to working-age contributors increases, the math starts to work against us. To keep even on our current promises, we'll likely have to raise our ongoing contribution rate of 12.4 percent by at least 2 percent and also increase the amount of income subject to Social Security taxes (currently, incomes up to $137,700 are subject to the tax).

In addition to tax-advantaged individual retirement accounts (IRAs)—only about 23 percent of Americans have one of these—the other major way we save for retirement in the United States is through pension accounts sponsored by many employers, known as 401(k) plans. Employees can designate a certain part of their salary to be contributed to this tax-advantaged retirement savings account, and some employers provide an additional match of a portion of the employee's contribution. As with IRAs, employees typically have many options for investing the money.

There's only one problem with all of this.

The people who need retirement accounts the most don't have them. For the most part, these programs are voluntary. Most people at lower incomes have more immediate needs than saving for retirement. According to EPI, "nearly nine in 10 families in the top income fifth had retirement account savings, compared with fewer than one in 10 families in the bottom income fifth." Only 26 percent of Hispanic families and 41 percent of black families have retirement account savings. Even for black and Hispanic families *with* retirement account savings, the median amount saved is only $22,000—almost insignificant relative to actual retirement needs.

So, what can we do? You see where I'm going here. How about just copying Australia? Instead of contributing to Social Security, let's divert all of those Social Security taxes to personal retirement accounts like the superannuation accounts that Australians have! That way everyone can start saving and investing as soon as they start working. Remember those compound interest tables, Investor A and Investor B. Getting started early is the key. "Stealing" those Social Security taxes from the beginning of an employee's working career and investing them at higher rates of return than U.S. government bonds (while simultaneously supporting increased investment in the private economy) could potentially be a game changer for those who need it the most when retirement comes around.

As long as we're just spitballing here, what if we also increased the limit on how we assess Social Security taxes. For 2020, the Social Security tax is only assessed on the first $137,700 of income. Why does it stop there? The reason goes back to the original purpose of Social Security. It was designed as a retirement savings program (with some disability insurance attached). Although those at lower income levels get a proportionately larger payout relative to contributions than higher-income participants, Social Security largely sticks to the original notion that what you get out of the program is closely related to your contributions over the years. To preserve that relationship, since Social Security payouts are capped, so are contributions, and that's where the current $137,700 limit comes from.

If we continue to assess Social Security taxes on those earning more than $137,700 without providing increased retirement benefits, that original relationship between contributions and payouts will be broken. In other words, it would be just like raising tax rates on workers with higher incomes. That may be fine but that decision to raise tax rates should be unrelated to Social Security. If it's just an increase in tax rates, why shouldn't we spend the increased tax receipts on helping with childhood poverty, education budgets, better infrastructure, or just name your priority? Why should the benefits of those higher taxes go solely to retirees?

So, here's why I'm suggesting we keep assessing Social Security taxes beyond the current $137,700 limit. I just proposed we consider changing the nature of Social Security. The 12.4 percent we are currently assessed on wages won't be taxes anymore. These assessments will become contributions to our own superannuation-like retirement account. But rather than just another tax-advantaged retirement account that mostly benefits the relatively well-off, here's what we can do. For the amounts assessed on incomes above $137,700, not all of that extra contribution will go into the high earner's superannuation-like account. Some portion of their contributions, perhaps 15 or 20 percent, will be taken upfront and immediately placed in the accounts of workers earning less than $137,700 based on a formula that favors those at lower income levels.

The compounding benefits for younger and/or lower-income workers receiving these supplemental contributions could be enormous over time. For high earners, these accounts will still maintain tax advantages that should overcome the effects of immediately taking 15 or 20 percent of their contributions off the top to supplement other people's retirement accounts. Yes, we will still need a safety net like

Australia's Age Pension (especially during the next few decades) that makes up the difference between currently promised Social Security benefits and what income these new retirement accounts can provide. But the bottom line should be this: Everyone will be guaranteed retirement benefits that are at least as generous as our current promises under Social Security.

So, what's wrong with this new plan to "privatize" Social Security? In short, so much—I don't know where to get started. But let's start with this: Most people are bad investors. It's not even close. Expecting individuals to make hundreds of good investment choices over a period of decades in their new private retirement accounts instead of simply continuing to earn benefits through our current Social Security program could turn out very badly.

In 2005, I published a book (*The Little Book That Beats the Market*) featuring a simple formula to pick stocks that encapsulated the most important principles I use when making my own stock selections. Let's ignore whether the formula is good or not; hundreds of readers asked for more help in managing their portfolios using the methods in the book. So, I had an idea.

It was based on an idea I had long ago about creating a "benevolent" brokerage firm that sought to protect its customers from the most common investing errors. The firm would still let clients pick individual stocks, but those stocks would have to be selected from a preapproved list based on the principles and formula outlined in the book. We would encourage clients to hold a portfolio of at least 20 to 30 stocks from this list to help create a diversified portfolio and we would send them reminders to make trades at the proper time based on the plan in the book. To make sure customers could pursue this investment strategy over the long term, we wouldn't allow margin accounts (borrowing). We called these accounts "self-managed."

At the last minute, we decided to give customers an additional choice: they could just check a box that essentially said "Just do this for me." This version, which we dubbed a "professionally managed" account, would follow a pre-planned system to buy top-ranked stocks from the list at periodic intervals. No judgment involved—just automatically buy the list and follow the plan.

What was the result? In short, an unintended experiment across thousands of investment accounts. As it turned out, the self-managed accounts, where clients could choose their own stocks from the preapproved list and then follow (or not) our guidelines for trading the stocks at fixed intervals didn't do too badly. A compilation of all self-managed accounts for the two-year period after we started showed a cumulative return of 59.4 percent after all expenses. Not too bad—except that the S&P 500 during the same period was up 62.7 percent.

But a compilation of the "professionally managed" accounts that just automatically followed the rules earned 84.1 percent after all expenses over the same two years, beating the "self-managed" by almost 25 percent (and the S&P by well over 20 percent). For just a two-year period, that's a huge difference. It's especially huge since both "self-managed" and "professionally managed" accounts chose investments from the same list of stocks and supposedly followed the same basic game plan.

One conclusion could be that on average the people who self-managed their accounts took a good plan and used their judgment to unintentionally eliminate all the outperformance and then some. Looking more closely through the accounts, here's what appeared to happen:

1. Self-managed investors avoided buying many of the biggest winners—most likely because the biggest winners are usually the most out-of-favor companies that are psychologically difficult to buy. Many self-managed investors eliminated companies from the list that they just knew from reading the newspaper faced a near-term problem or uncertainty. But many of these companies turned out to be the biggest future winners.

2. Many self-managed investors stopped following the book's game plan *after* the strategy underperformed or the market fell for a period of time. Why? Probably because it's hard to stick with a strategy that's not working for a little while or to hang in there when the market drops. Yet, these same investors put more money into the strategy only *after* it outperformed or the market went up.

Look no further than the best-performing U.S. stock mutual fund for the decade of the 2000s to confirm this wasn't a fluke. This best-performing fund actually earned over 18 percent per year over the decade while the popular market averages were essentially flat. However, because investors bailed out during the periods *after* the fund had underperformed or the market went down and put in more money only *after* the fund had outperformed or the market went up, the average investor (weighted by dollars invested) actually turned the fund's 18 percent annual gain into an average annual *loss* of 11 percent during the same ten-year period.

Another way to think about all this:

Investing is hard. Maybe privatizing Social Security isn't such a good idea.

But that's not the only problem. Diverting Social Security taxes directly to private accounts would mean that we would no longer have that money to give to current Social Security beneficiaries. This money would have to be borrowed by the government to meet the Social Security benefit promises we've already made—hundreds of billions of dollars in added borrowing each year.

Of course, similar to Australia, over time our new private retirement accounts should eliminate some, if not all, of our future obligations under Social Security. This would take decades. But eventually, if the new private retirement accounts provided income to retirees that equals or exceeds currently promised Social Security benefits, the government would be relieved of this long-term obligation. If the returns on private accounts exceeded the returns from U.S. government bonds (the cost of borrowing the money to pay current Social Security obligations), then this could be a win for everyone.

There are plenty of other complications that would come along with this privatization plan, but back to the real world for a minute. People love Social Security. In a heavily politicized environment, it would be next to impossible to reach a consensus on changing a program that has worked well for so many over decades. Although at the current Social Security tax rate we will not have enough funding in fifteen years to meet our promised benefits under the current program, this shortfall will likely be addressed in a conventional way. Social Security tax rates will eventually be increased several points above the current 12.4 percent rate, the cap on incomes (currently set at $137,700) will be raised to a limited degree, and perhaps the ages of eligibility for Social Security benefits will be raised slightly over time. And that's that.

But what can we do for those retirees who will be left with only their Social Security checks? Our current system isn't very generous and doesn't get the job done for seniors who have little or no retirement savings. Over the coming decades, unless we change our retirement savings policies or habits, that will likely be true for most Americans.

Two ideas.

First, without changing anything for most people, we can just supplement our current Social Security program with a private savings plan. The private plan would be financed by increasing the cap on Social Security taxes for high earners (above the current $137,700 income level or the prevailing cap at the time of enactment). However, the amount "taxed" above the prevailing cap would not go to the government. Instead, the additional "taxes" would go to private retirement accounts.

As with the previously described plan, 15 to 20 percent of these new "taxes" on high earners would come off the top and go directly to the private retirement accounts of those earning under $137,700, favoring those at the lowest income levels. The rest would be left in retirement accounts for the high earners. The tax benefits of these accounts should compensate for the 15 or 20 percent taken off the top. This plan would have the advantage of keeping the underlying nature of the current Social Security program, where benefits remain mostly proportional to contributions, while immediately providing new retirement accounts for lower-wage workers that could compound over time.

The second idea would be similar but it would not be compulsory like the Social Security–based plan. Here, we would make use of our current 401(k) system. For 2020, employees are limited to annual contributions into a 401(k) plan of $19,500 (about $6,000 higher for employees already over 50). We could lift this limit for high earners but "tax" these added contributions upfront, so that 15–20 percent of these contributions would be directed into the accounts of those at lower income levels.

Once again, the tax benefits of the retirement accounts for high earners would theoretically make up for this 15–20 percent upfront tax. As opposed to the compulsory nature of Social Security taxes, these additional contributions by high earners would be voluntary. For this plan to work, however, employers would have to set up and administer mandatory 401(k) accounts for all employees (a good thing).

(If you are worried about tax breaks for the rich in either the Social Security or 401(k) plans, the upfront 15–20 percent tax could be raised and the tax benefits for the retirement accounts of high earners could be adjusted to levels deemed fair and appropriate.)

Okay, but what about the problem that most people aren't great at investing? While I am generally in favor of private retirement accounts and investor choice, mainly so that workers at lower income levels have the opportunity to earn higher compounded returns than government bonds and more investment is made in the private economy, I believe these investment choices should be limited. My suggestion: fewer than ten choices of widely diversified, professionally managed retirement accounts consisting primarily of indexes and low-cost funds across major asset classes.

If workers did not make a choice, their retirement account would be defaulted into an appropriate account based on age. Account managers would be chosen by the government to construct widely diversified portfolios at varying risk levels. Managers would be selected through a transparent process and require re-approval every seven to ten years.

But forget all the details for now. Let's get back to the simplicity of ninth grade. Investing early in a disciplined manner is the key to taking advantage of the magic of compounding. For the most part, as a society we are blowing it. This is particularly true for the bottom half of wage earners.

The best opportunity we have to provide a comfortable retirement for our citizens is to use our existing Social Security system as a base and add onto it. If we simply raise taxes further, more retirement savings will be just one of the many legitimate needs calling out for the additional funding. But we clearly need a new plan.

Whatever plan we choose—Australia's or some version that rhymes with Australia (rhyming with superannuation is too hard)—the sooner we act, the sooner the power of compound investing can start changing the math for those who are currently destined to miss out on a fair and livable retirement.

CONCLUSION

In the documentary movie *The Gatekeepers*, Ami Ayalon, former commander-in-chief of the Israeli Navy and head of Israel's equivalent of the FBI (the Shin Bet), recounts that when he was a child he always believed that somewhere "in Jerusalem, on the second floor of an office building, there is a long corridor with a door at the end, and behind that door is a wise man making wise decisions for Israel." But now that he's older, Ayalon shares wistfully, "I've been to that building and walked down that corridor and there is no door at the end of it, and no wise man behind that door doing the necessary thinking on my behalf."

Of course, we'd all love it if we knew that someone in charge, both wise and kind, was making all the important decisions for us and our nation. But while getting older comes with a loss of naïveté and an increase in responsibility, it can also come with a sense of empowerment. "Never doubt that a small group of thoughtful, committed citizens can change the world. Indeed, it is the only thing that ever has," said Margaret Mead. And hopefully she's still right.

But recently, it hasn't seemed that way. Writing this book in the midst of a paralyzing and destructive political environment has made me think that Paul Simon nailed our current predicament fifty years ago when he sang (ironically, in perfect two-part harmony), "Still a man hears what he wants to hear—And disregards the rest." While nothing new, the "not hearing" on both sides feels like it has reached historic levels.

Yet, there are some principles and ideals that remain so universal that there should be few impediments daunting enough to prevent us from continuing to work toward them. You don't have to be an investor to realize that the biggest payoff of all would come from ensuring that all of the youngest members of our society get a great education. Everyone believes that. Only, we don't act that way. We systematically send our poor and minority children to the worst schools.

That's not okay. But offering those children and parents another choice, something called a "charter school," has become a trigger where people immediately take sides and stop focusing on solving the problem. Fine—some charters clearly provide a better choice and some don't. Maybe we should encourage the ones that do. But if not, a study across one million students led by Harvard researcher Raj Chetty suggests that replacing a bottom-5-percent teacher with even an average teacher would "increase the present value of students' lifetime income by approximately $250,000 per classroom." Students moved to a better teacher "are more likely to attend college, earn higher salaries, and are less likely to have children as teenagers."

So, what should we do when children from poor and low-income families are assigned to an entire school that for years has been in the bottom 5 or 10 percent? Given our lack of success in improving these schools, shouldn't we be required to give students another choice right now? Maybe a guaranteed spot in the nearest school ranked in the top half?

An investor's mind begins to spin with the possibilities. Since, by definition, there would always be schools at the bottom, how long could we keep the cycle going? Wouldn't parents already zoned for the best schools object? And maybe, if their children started getting displaced, would they then start aggressively supporting better schools or good charter options for the low-income kids near them? If all went well, maybe poor schools and poor choices for low-income families would suddenly become everyone's problem to solve.

Investors walk down the street and certainly see which stores are the busiest and which cars the most popular. But they are also trying to figure out how incentives are set up and what's likely to happen next as a result. And while viewing the world like an investor still has me concerned about our traditional education system, it has me very excited about the potential for *alternative certification*.

If specific standards were set by top employers trying to fill available jobs without requiring a traditional degree, it seems wholly reasonable that a supportive ecosystem of online resources, tutoring services, and targeted courses would soon develop to meet this new demand. For those not ready to take the specified exam or course due to missed opportunities or a poor education, a supportive ecosystem of prerequisite resources would also likely develop. Most important, no entrenched interests could stop this from happening. No consensus would be needed for such a system to work, only the willingness of employers to set clear standards. And all of this could be jumpstarted right now.

For those adults who aren't in a position to take advantage of more education or more training at this time, greatly expanding our existing *earned income tax credit* could provide tremendous benefits. A good-paying job for everyone willing to work is also a universal principle that everyone would support if only we could afford it. From a long-term investor's standpoint, the reduction in childhood poverty and adult medical expenses would make the costs of this expansion less than free. At less than free, we can.

Sadly, in today's charged political environment, the word "immigration" has also become a trigger word. But what if we changed the term "skilled immigration" to "Hey, there's a free gold mine over there!"? Would it make sense for the response to be "I'm not filling up my wheelbarrow with free gold until you solve the refugee issue first!"? Frankly speaking, I don't know any investors who would think so (as they pushed me aside racing toward the gold). It would be a complete non sequitur. Yes, we should develop coherent and generous policies for Dreamers and unskilled immigrants seeking a better life, but that has nothing to do with whether we should accept all the free money, jobs, and economic growth a smart skilled-immigration policy would bring.

And then we subsidize banks—big bad banks! We do it by helping to guarantee their deposits. Get over it. Like it or not, it's good for all of us. But let's get the full benefit. If we subsidize the cost of their deposits, at least we should benefit by having banks lend to small businesses and individuals at attractive rates that reflect those subsidies. Regulate them too much and their costs and lending rates go up. Penalize them for lending to small businesses and individual borrowers and they'll do less of it and charge higher prices. But having investors bear most of the risks, rather than taxpayers, will be better for everyone.

Let's see. More equity capital for banks, less need for regulation, more and cheaper loans for small businesses and individuals, plus less risk for taxpayers—all from a new type of preferred stock. Who woulda thunk it?

Lastly, our country's retirement game plan needs to change. For the most part, it doesn't work for the bottom half of earners. Social Security isn't nearly enough and voluntary participation in private savings plans, IRAs, and 401(k)s works best for those already at the top end.

As every investor knows, the solution lies in the magic of compounding. Everyone needs to start saving in a disciplined way as early as possible. Given the budget demands for the bottom half of earners and for those just beginning to work, this means we need a new strategy that adds discipline and a helping hand starting early on. Australia has an interesting plan; we need one too.

According to John Adams, "Without the pen of the author of 'Common Sense,' the sword of Washington would have been raised in vain." Words matter. Ideas matter. If the cause is important enough, people care. We all want more equality and more opportunity for our citizens. We all want to grow the economic pie for the benefit of everyone. The more ideas we share, the more discussion we have and the less fighting we engage in, the faster we'll reach our mutual goals. That's just common sense.